Californication:
The Rise of the American Technocracy

ISBN 13c: 978-1-7359851-0-7

Table of Contents

technocracy / tek-nok-ruh-see

n.

The government or control of society or industry by an elite of technical experts.

Oxford English Dictionary

Introduction

After obtaining a Bachelor of Arts degree in History, I found the culture in America's educational system to be oppressive and divisive. I felt that my skills would be better utilized in the periphery. Throughout my professional career during and after college, I was surprised to find that the America I knew growing up no longer existed. Entering the market right as the 2008 recession reached its peak changed my perspective forever, and it forced me to think of new possibilities while studying world history and American history. Simultaneously, while studying and working in Denver, Colorado, all I could do was watch as the cost of living skyrocketed, and neighborhoods continued to decline with homelessness increasing across the front range. There was an underlying problem that I was not aware of yet. It was as if Colorado's transformation was part of a larger plan to destroy the American middle-class.

My short career in the hospitality industry during college allowed me to travel and see America. I was able to compare and contrast the socioeconomic situations of each city and state I traveled to. Being a Colorado native, most of this travel was out West. As a kid, I loved the thought of moving to California. In college, I would visit Los Angeles every Christmas to see my L.A. Lakers play at the Staples Center, followed by a Disneyland trip. My most recent visit was after my political position had been solidified. I could see the destruction the City of Los Angeles had undergone in the trips I had taken from 2009-2015. The homelessness that seemed restricted to L.A.'s infamous "Skid Row" had spread like fast-moving cancer across the city. Where there was once thriving businesses and clean streets, there is now filth, tents, and Bernie Sanders murals.

Throughout California, the destruction that I saw I also found in other cities. In my trip across the country through Chicago, there were literal no-go zones due to rampant crime and tent cities spreading blocks. Throughout America, something was causing the country to rip apart at its seams. It's as if common sense and human decency have all but disappeared. We no longer trust the government, we no longer trust our neighbor, and we no longer trust each other. Why?

I had to find the source of America's problems. Not only had the situation perturbed my inquisitive mind for understanding people and history, but the socioeconomic environment in the country was also beginning to have a negative impact on my life and the lives around me. The more *California* license plates I saw in Colorado, the more I noticed the destruction that had followed them. It was clear that these newcomers were bringing the policies that existed in California with them. I knew that to understand America's transformation, I had to understand California's political history. How and why did California go from a state that elected Ronald Reagan to *a Marxist hellhole?* More importantly, why did Colorado follow suit?

Since the COVID-19 outbreak, every major city has been hit with an economic recession, followed by political violence. Denver, Colorado, now looks like a scene out of Mel Gibson's "Mad Max." The same can be said of cities like Portland, Seattle, Washington, Chicago, and Baltimore. It seems as if the implementation of progressive policies has been rolled out with the government's reaction to the COVID-19 pandemic. Some will argue this is merely the logical reaction from government bureaucrats, others will argue that we are witnessing a national conspiracy.

Many people know of the statement, "History repeats itself." One of my professors used to like to say, "History doesn't repeat itself, but it definitely rhymes." To illustrate the difference between the two, we can look at the historical interpretations of the Nazi regime of the 1930s and 40s. Historians that adhere to the first statement would teach that fascism and Nazism are wrong, and the philosophy should never be allowed to exist again. They will formulate this conclusion by observing the core tenets and programs of the Nazi philosophy and follow up by asserting that if fascism returns, it will look and act identical to the Nazi German form of fascism. It is a black-and-white analysis of historical events.

The second statement lives in the gray. It acknowledges that although certain trends and ideas change, there seems to be a cyclical pattern of oppression, starvation, war, and economic instability. It recognizes that these cycles can impact all types of political systems and belief systems. From this perspective, historians and political scientists will acknowledge that the form of fascism the Nazis spread across Europe in the 1930s will likely be sold in a different package if it returns. No matter the historical era, political opportunists will use political labels to exploit certain policies to advance their agenda, always sacrificing one group while uplifting another. The same can be said for the collapse of communism and capitalism. It is the job of historians and political scientists alike to connect these ideologies with specific patterns and develop a consensus as to the real source of humanity's problems. All political systems fail, it is the task of a historian to help us comprehend why. An understanding must be developed to find the most reliable political system for maintaining individual liberty and a stable society.

From my perspective, humanity's letdowns can be summarized under one word: *collectivization.* When we look at the major political systems of the 20th century, any time we see full collectivization of power, things always fall apart. We saw this with the rogue monopolies of the late 19th century and early 20th century. We saw it again in the form of "National Socialism" under Adolf Hitler and communism with Vladimir Lenin and Joseph Stalin in the mid-20th century. When dissecting these power structures further, you find that they were instigated by the same corrupt interests and maintained with the respective government's permission. This observation allows one to view social uprisings and the inevitable structural change that follows with a different perspective.

The purpose of *Californication: The Rise of the American Technocracy* is to warn you of the impending cycle change for the 21st century that America and the world are currently undergoing. The same global interests that dictated world events in the 20th century are working to shake up the table so that they continue to hold the cards. The new economic and political system that will result will redefine America's standard of living forever.

7

America's addiction to government intervention has served as the perfect petri dish for their plan. This book does not merely offer the popular dissertation of gloom-and-doom that many present in politics. Instead, this book will provide solutions to help Americans combat the United Nations Agenda 2030 program while maintaining their individual and national sovereignty. Ultimately, the mainline historical narrative must have a conscientious objector.

In this analysis, you will learn about: America's Founding Fathers and the philosophers who inspired them, constitutional rights, property rights, the economic crash of 2008, COVID-19 and its true intentions, communism, cultural Marxism, and the Agenda 2030 technocratic program. By the end of the book, you will have learned how to readily explain the Declaration of Independence and the Constitution's true intentions. Simultaneously, defects of the Constitution will be highlighted so that proper steps are taken to reduce the size of the bureaucratic state. My goal is to offer hope for humanity's future while living in the technetronic era by providing viable solutions for the average man.

For Liberty,

Joseph Pendleton

I

The American Dream, or an American Nightmare?

"They'll get it all from you sooner or later. Because they own
this fuckin' place. It's a big club, and you ain't in it! It's called
the 'American Dream' because you have to be asleep to believe
it."
George Carlin

The United States of America once created the most expansive economic middle class in the world. Other countries envied the success of American citizens, and the term "American Dream" became popular. What is the definition of the "American Dream?" Is this definition the same for everyone? The underlying themes among the American populace are similar but always remain unique for each individual. Americans focus on things like the ability to create a family, own a home and car, and to use their disposable income for exotic vacations. If you were to ask an economist what the "American Dream" was, they would present data and statistics along with charts and graphs to argue the necessary income to reach middle-class status. They say, "Once you reach this point, you've made it, kid." The average American simply wants a balanced lifestyle that rewards individuals for hard work, and if that type of opportunity exists, most feel the financials would presumably be covered. It is vital to recognize when these goals become out of reach financially as debt can become an insurmountable hurdle.

Without a doubt, scholars argue a certain level of self-reliance must be reached: the ability to create and invent, the ability to own a home and earn equity, the ability to save financially, and the ability to utilize disposable income are all necessary qualities in a sustainable market. Many would also argue the power to stop working and enjoy one's fruits of labor is the overall goal as economic mobility represents the crux of the American lifestyle. Yet, it seems as if people ignore the political functions required to maintain a financial system that helps people reach these goals. All of these themes rely on the concept of freedom of choice. This narrative aims to provide a clear presentation of which political and economic concepts uphold the American dream and which do not. Overall, the idea of the "American Dream" can be summarized in two words: individual liberty. Political ideologies that constrain personal freedom have always posed a direct threat to the economic mobility Americans value most.

History has shown that economic mobility for citizens in a country tends to mirror the human rights record. Arguably, the United States has modeled its form of government based on this truth. While there are ideologies that uphold American ideals, there are also schools of philosophy that pose a direct threat to Americans' economic and social prosperity. To accurately illustrate this point, it is necessary to analyze the original writings of classical philosophers like Plato and other political theorists that followed him. By comparing and contrasting the profound ideas that form the basis for individual freedom, the difference between the United States formula of government and others becomes apparent. How much individual freedom one has is dependent upon the political ideology they adhere to. In the end, it is clear that all political ideologies have diverged along a spectrum with individuality on one end, and all-embracing collectivism on the other. America was founded on the concept that individuals are sovereign with inalienable rights. Political and social collectivism was ultimately viewed as a threat to individual liberty. That fact is evident in the United States' founding documents born out of the classical liberal ideologies that preceded them.

The difficulty of creating a finite definition of the "American Dream" has continually agitated the country for its entire 241-year history. After all, it has always been a complex operation to create and maintain a national identity for any country in the world. Shortly after America's founding, venture capitalists, politicians, and theologians alike surmised that America's destiny was to expand to the west coast while providing freedom and prosperity to its citizens abroad. The proclamation of "Manifest Destiny" was one of the earliest examples of American exceptionalism. It would be hypocritical and contradictory to promote this theory while not demanding economic progress for its people. Of course, politicians and citizens alike would debate what type of economic and political system is the most efficient in this regard.

It took many political battles through legal means and an eventual civil war to form the government we know of today. Ultimately, historians and economists tend to agree that the United States' format for the Constitutional Democratic Republic maintains the most robust environment for individual liberty and economic prosperity. It allowed individuals to thrive in an atmosphere where private property was respected, allowing them to earn and hold the financial rewards from their labor. There is no denying that America has set the standard when it comes to individual property rights. The discussions about the inherent connection between property rights and human rights helped America's Founding Fathers craft the Declaration of Independence and only eleven years later, the US Constitution. We will examine the importance of property ownership rights and how they were necessary to hold necessary human rights early on. Undoubtedly, it will become clear that property rights and individual liberty go hand in hand. These ideas would help form towns and cities with a legal and physical framework to guide the creation and maintenance of roads, bridges, schools, and later, utilities like water and electricity. And all of this would be created through volunteered consent written in the form of legal contracts.

Indisputably, America's founding paved the way for creating a government that helped foster the growth of the world's largest economic middle class. The founders built a government that addressed the will of the people by protecting every citizen's individual rights. They understood the philosophical arguments proposed by classical liberals that individuals must hold title to the property they earn from their labor. By protecting these rights, citizens have a vested interest in their survival, their community's survival, and their government.

Unfortunately, in the 20th century, the rise of political and social collectivism throughout American society has seemingly mirrored the increase in social inequality and economic volatility. Undoubtedly, these circumstances pose a direct threat to the American way of life. This is evidenced in America's addiction to creating government programs for every possible economic, political, or social problem. Ultimately, these programs hinder American prosperity as they tend to exacerbate the exact problem they intended to avoid. As more questions reveal themselves, more programs are created, which cause more problems—and the process continues like a revolving door. The majority of government bureaucracies operate based on communist and socialist political ideologies that support the thesis that society must be maintained by a technological oligarchy. Although communists and socialists differ in several ways, they always keep the notion that a group of specialists must regulate a nation's economy. They typically argue that any societal matter should be handled by people they deem as specialists. In their view, the collectivization of power is necessary to enforce the proper distribution of wealth to construct and maintain a civil society. How else can disaster be avoided?

America has always experienced populist movements that promoted collectivist political ideologies like socialism or communism, especially concerning worker's rights in the late 19th century. In this circumstance, the collectivist argument for increased government influence in the relationship between workers and business owners helped raise labor standards for the American worker. Labor unions are credited with establishing child labor laws and the 8-hour workweek. Since then, socialist organizations have transitioned their focus to the problem of poverty by demanding equal economic outcomes for all workers. By fully adopting socialist and communist principles on economic theory, politicians ultimately abandoned the classical liberal philosophies that America was built upon.

The creation of the Federal Reserve Banking System in 1913 changed the American economy entirely. It was designed by followers and supporters of Keynesian economic theory who believe a macro-level financial manager is necessary to help the country avoid hard recessions while reaching a certain level of economic equilibrium. On the contrary, the Federal Reserve System and its short 100-year history have provided multiple financial crises for the American people, starting with the Great Depression beginning in 1929 that ended in 1937, the recessions of 1973 and 1981-82, the 1987 stock market crash, the 2000 tech bubble, and more recently, 2008's "Great Recession." Each of these economic periods had unemployment rates that were at least eight percent or higher when considering those who have stopped looking for work. The Great Depression saw unemployment rates of twenty-five percent.[1] If we examine the periods between these hard recessions, we will also see other economic relapses that surely do not reflect a sustainable economy. Overall, the Federal

---

[1] "Unemployment Rate," FRED Economic Data (Federal Reserve of St. Louis), accessed March 5, 2020, https://fred.stlouisfed.org/search?st=Unemployment Rate for United States)

Reserve has a strong history of violent boom and bust cycles. With these examples in mind, it is crucial to examine why these sharp increases and matching declines keep happening while getting worse as time progresses. When looking at the United States' full economic history, one could argue the only time of consistent, sustainable growth was during the Industrial Revolution and directly after World War Two.[2] Although these economic booms were historic, the volatile cycles marked between these periods are a direct result of poor management of the economy, from a chosen group of specialists.

In response to the Federal Reserve's mismanagement of the United States economy, President Franklin Delano Roosevelt championed his New Deal legislation as the national cure. It recommended more financial regulation and welfare programs like Social Security, to ensure people always have a solid footing in the economy. Moving past the New Deal era from 1932 to 1938, Keynesian economists and socialist-leaning city planners found their most potent ally in the environmental movement that found a stronger foothold during the late sixties' civil rights era. Similar to FDR's policies on the national economy, environmentalists also felt America must create federal regulatory bodies to ensure environmental needs are considered when conducting business. The "precautionary principle," as they call it, promoted the theory that environmental protection must be considered in all human affairs. Broadly, the precautionary principle promotes the approach that there are some risks where consequences are not realized until a much later date, and we must find ways to prevent these future calamities in the present time. Although this idea is touted as something new, it is still based on the communist and socialist ideologies touted by theorists like Karl Marx and Friedrich Engels. Nevertheless, political collectivists continue to promote the notion that more management by educated specialists will cure all socioeconomic ailments. In their minds, if there is a problem, it was the result of poor management or not enough direction; admitting to the fact that the problem is not manageable at all would require them to relinquish their control.

More recently, with economic data proving a historic

2 Jordan Weissmann, "60 Years of American Economic History, Told in 1 Graph," The Atlantic (Atlantic Media Company, September 6, 2012), https://www.theatlantic.com/business/archive/2012/08/60-years-of-american-economic-history-told-in-1-graph/261503/)

decline in the size of the middle class[3], many have questioned whether the American Dream is reachable for future generations. Over the last thirty years, manufacturing and exporting has declined significantly for the United States.[4]This trend has continued with multiple crises from the tech bubble of 2000 to the housing crisis in 2008 that caused over 10 million foreclosures nationwide. At the height of the Great Recession in 2008, the national foreclosure rate was just over 3 percent[5]—2% higher than the foreclosure rate at the peak of the Great Depression in 1933.[6] This event was labeled as the "Great Recession." Perhaps naming it "The Great Depression 2" was too much of a cliché for the American people. The Great Recession in 2008 changed the working definitions of critical economic functions throughout America. The problems that preceded the collapse were exposed, and more importantly, the purported solutions that followed redefined the economic landscape in America forever. The term "Bailout" immediately comes to mind. Say goodbye to large banking institutions going broke, even if they caused the economic collapse in the first place. United States financial controllers felt these institutions were integral to keeping the global market intact and could not fail. When examining the aspects of the housing crisis of 2007-08, evidence will be provided to show that the inherent flaws in the market functions were not fixed or replaced. They were augmented in scope, and the changes that were made have only exacerbated these same problems. Does this sound familiar?

Although many mainline analysts argue the rise in the stock market over the last ten years represents a rise in the national economy, the data does not support that thesis. The response by the US Congress and Federal Reserve only buried the fundamental flaws in the market that caused the 2008 recession. The

[3] "The American Middle Class Is Losing Ground," Pew Research Center's Social & Demographic Trends Project, December 31, 2019, http://www.pewsocialtrends.org/2015/12/09/the-american-middle-class-is-losing-ground/)

[4] "History shows that trade made easy, "US Has Lost 5 Million Manufacturing Jobs since 2000," CNNMoney (Cable News Network), accessed March 5, 2020, http://money.cnn.com/2016/03/29/news/economy/us-manufacturing-jobs/)

[5] William R. Emmons, "The End Is in Sight for the US Foreclosure Crisis," Federal Reserve Bank of St. Louis (Federal Reserve Bank of St. Louis, December 14, 2016), https://www.stlouisfed.org/publications/housing-market-perspectives/2016/the-end-is-in-sight-for-the-us-foreclosure-crisis#endnote1)

[6] David C Wheelock, "The Federal Response to Home Mortgage Distress: Lessons from the Great Depression," Federal Reserve Bank of St. Louis Review, 2008, pp. 133-148, https://files.stlouisfed.org/files/htdocs/publications/review/08/05/Wheelock.pdf, p.137)

labor participation rate throughout this purported recovery period lies at a historically low rate of 64 percent.[7] The average income of Americans has yet to rise to match the true level of inflation.[8] These facts, among others, prove that this is one of the worst recoveries in American history, as we will highlight in the coming chapters. Ultimately, the marriage between Congress and the Federal Reserve system is once again to blame for these problems. Printing money with historically low-interest rates will undoubtedly cause another unsustainable bubble that always has to burst. Yet, those who still support the big lies promoted by Keynesian economists believe they can manage their way out of the next economic correction. Overall, increased political collectivization has led to more socioeconomic problems for America; it has not led to the romantic prosperity they have always promised.

In the discussions that followed the severe economic downturn of 2008, financial and political discourse turned nasty. Friends were turned against friends, husbands against wives, neighbors against neighbors. Everyone thought they had the answer as to why the Great Recession had occurred and what we could do to avoid economic disaster in the future. These debates turned into arguments and eventually led to the "Occupy Wall Street" movement. Americans focused their rage on those who permitted and committed acts of fraud that led to the destruction of millions of American jobs, bank accounts, and retirement funds. Simultaneously, the tea party movement also significantly impacted the midterm elections that followed President Obama's election. The debate between collectivists, who argued for more government, and individualists, who promoted less, rose to the forefront of American politics. No one knew where to place the blame, as the problem was so complicated. And those who did could do nothing about it. No one went to jail, and if fines were assessed, they were minuscule in the grand scheme of things. For the people who lost their jobs and eventually their homes, there was no recourse. It is obvious to see why political polarization

[7] "Labor Force Participation Rate," US Bureau of Labor Statistics (US Bureau of Labor Statistics), accessed March 12, 2020, https://data.bls.gov/)

[8] Drew DeSilver, "For Most Americans, Real Wages Have Barely Budged for Decades," Pew Research Center (Pew Research Center, August 7, 2018), http://www.pewresearch.org/fact-tank/2014/10/09/for-most-workers-real-wages-have-barely-budged-for-decades/)

today is at an all-time high.[9]

The data observed from the 2008 recession will shed light on the collapse of many American cities, and even states. As the disintegration of cities like Baltimore, Chicago, Detroit, and New Orleans continues, a new economic structure will be created out of the ashes. These residents are compelled to flee their homes to cities and states that have more robust markets. The question is, will these cities ever recover? Or are they meant to fall, as if the new city planners and politicians have a different type of reconstruction in mind? To properly move forward with real results for the American people, it is necessary to examine our leaders' plans and remedies currently being presented. Mostly, many of these ideas were founded in schools of thought that are not new. They are old and tired with a strong record of failure, rebranded for the next generation of socialist political scientists and city planners. One has to ask whether America's recurring socioeconomic problems are simply an excuse to increase government control over the market and its participants.

So, has the Federal Reserve board managed the economy without negative consequences? We know FDR would not have promoted his socialist New Deal legislation had it been so. Did his legislation fix the national economy for good? Our analysis will illustrate that the United States' increased dependence on socialist economic policies has increased volatility, rather than curb it. In recent times, there is a misplaced belief that free-market capitalism is to blame, instead of the outright fraud perpetrated against the American people. Overall, it is self-evident that constant government regulation has a strong record of causing more problems than preventing them, but Americans still clamor for more of it. The precautionary principle has redefined our response to difficulties concerning socioeconomics and the environment. In today's current form, there is no separating the two. Consequently, it has entirely redefined America's governmental structure and culture.

The recent rise in popularity for socialism and communism is not a fluke. Whether leftist political scientists want to acknowledge it or not, it is undeniable that America has been on an upward socialist trend since the Federal Reserve's creation in

---

[9] Hannah Fingerhut, "Partisanship and Political Animosity in 2016," Pew Research Center for the People and the Press, December 31, 2019, http://www.people-press.org/2016/06/22/partisanship-and-political-animosity-in-2016)

16

1913. The recent alliance between socialists and environmentalists in the early 1970s has led to a political and cultural revolution in the 21st century. Nongovernmental organizations, think-tanks, secret societies, and technology firms all have attached themselves to the environmental movement and vice versa. The ideologies they promote have infiltrated local city councils to effectively manage the economy, the building departments, zoning departments, and housing assistance programs throughout America. Representatives in Congress have also promoted socialist legislation on a national level. What do these programs all have in common? These initiatives aim to regulate your ability to participate in the market and own private property, core functions for a middle-class living. Furthermore, they are all based on collectivist political ideologies like communism and socialism. When compared to America's ideals, it is evident that these ideologies are not consistent with American laws or culture.

Determining a property's function is typically defined by zoning arrangements created by the local municipality. Our analysis will prove a strong relationship between forced scarcity and the multiple government institutions that currently exist at the local and national levels. Without a doubt, the home purchase process is complicated in America. One must question whether these processes are conducive to keeping prices relative to the home's actual market value or contributing to higher costs. The evidence will show that multiple government functions can either create equitable growth or wreak havoc in the housing market. Regulations either help an industry or destroy it, and typically it is the latter of the two. This analysis is vital to understanding the utilities of supply and demand and the overall impact on affordability. In the end, we will determine what truly sustains homeownership and the growth and maintenance of the middle class.

To fully understand how the precautionary principle and sustainable development affect the free-market and home affordability, it is fundamental that we look at the origins of the United Nations' Agenda 21 program (recently rebranded to Agenda 2030). The theories within Agenda 2030 suggest market volatility is a direct result of poor implementation of sustainable development programs.[10] Furthermore, the plans also imply a direct con-

[10] "Agenda 21" (United Nations, June 3, 1992), sustainabledevelopment.un.org/content/documents/Agenda21.pdf, Sec 1, Paragraph 3.1)

nection between global warming and economic crashes. These plans are primarily based on the theory of human-caused global warming and the potential economic and social disasters that will result. Some even list 2008's Great Recession as a consequence of climate change.[11] Of course, sustainable development planners offer economic solutions to mitigate perceived problems caused by the earth's climate. The discussion over whether these fears are founded will occur while also examining other potential solutions that do not exert unnecessary control on the market and its participants. Consequently, it will become evident that the precautionary principle has made its way into conceivably every regulatory framework within the US government.

Unfortunately, economists are finding that the implementation of these purported solutions ultimately results in higher costs for the average citizen, while creating more extensive patches of income inequality. The residential and commercial development that follows the implementation of Agenda 21 programs results in promoting more expensive apartments while not offering condos, townhomes, and family homes for individual ownership, which tends to help lower costs. The family homes that are built for ownership are often smaller, with less utility than previous designs. It also seems as though the enactment of sustainable development policies has coincided with the 2008 housing crash, where markets and banking institutions have hit the reset button. Are these plans merely another attempt to cause false demand and scarcity in the global market? More importantly, do these strategies promote individual and economic liberty? Or, is it possible these institutions are designed to destroy the concept of the "American Dream" altogether? Although the precautionary principle may have honest intentions, its use has become excessive. Many scholars believe that Agenda 21 and other programs like it are designed to inhibit human rights while also injuring the economy in ways that do not apply to the functions of free-market capitalism.

To accurately portray the changes in housing affordability across America for the average citizen, it is essential to look at specific cities as individual case studies. Many cities have experienced drastic changes due to extreme loss or gain in economic

---

[11] Henry M. Paulson Jr., "Opinion | The Coming Climate Crash," The New York Times (The New York Times, June 21, 2014), http://www.nytimes.com/2014/06/22/opinion/sunday/lessons-for-climate-change-in-the-2008-recession.html)

productivity due to the mismanagement of the national economy. For example, on the one hand, you have a city like Detroit, which used to lead the nation in automobile manufacturing before those companies chose to build overseas or next door in Canada or Mexico. The city is in ruins, infrastructure has collapsed, and crime has risen exponentially. On the other hand, you have cities like Denver, San Francisco, and Austin, Texas, who have experienced massive population influxes due to technological firms and other companies' investments. These cities have undergone many changes in infrastructure, culture, and population. Many economists and city planners would argue this is a direct consequence of natural population growth and new business development. However, others say that these changes are the direct consequence of strategic growth based on Agenda 2030 principles promoted under the guise of government initiatives, think-tanks and nongovernmental organizations, technological firms, and allied political organizations. In the end, both sentiments will prove to be accurate.

Out of all the cities that have experienced the most change, Denver, Colorado, has shown itself to be the centerpiece for future city planning in America. By examining documents and policy papers from government think-tanks, NGOs, and technology firms, it will become crystal clear that the growth of Denver and surrounding areas in Colorado is due to a planned change in the national economy. Denver, Colorado, will be one of the first of many "smart cities" built throughout America. These proposed changes are branded under the "Smart City" initiatives and other sustainable development programs. Each program has roots in policy papers based on the framework of the United Nations' Agenda 2030 plans. Overall, Denver, Colorado, serves as the best case study due to the amount of financial investment pouring into the state for smart city initiatives from government and private entities.

Additionally, Colorado's central geographic location in America has proven to be very attractive for tech firms as centralization in economic markets increases. As cities fall, new "megacities" are being created. This trend has increased due to financial consolidation and globalization in American markets, which have largely ignored the local manufacturing, agricultural, and energy industries throughout the Midwest and Northeast.

As new smart cities are built, technological companies

and governments have worked hand in hand to establish an entirely different type of socioeconomic infrastructure. Ideas like walkable communities with large bike lane networks and smaller traffic lanes are often coupled with small battery-operated rental cars, rentable bikes, and the new and trendy user-operated car services like Uber or Lyft. There is less focus on individual ownership and more of a focus on what is convenient or fashionable, forcing people into rental markets. As transportation and industry become more centralized with economies solely based on computer technology, surrounding rural markets are often left behind politically, economically, and socially. Increased automation from recent technological advancement will continually pose a threat to global job markets. We are also finding that technology has made people more isolated and infringes upon privacy with consequences yet to be realized. When we see the relationship between tech companies and government flourish, we are ultimately watching the implementation of a full-fledged technocracy.

Through and through, Agenda 2030 will be implemented through an established technocratic order based on property consolidation, forced scarcity, and behavior control. The technocratic order being built throughout many of America's cities and states has led to increased political and social disruption. This disruption is a direct result of rapid market changes resulting in larger swaths of income inequality nationwide. Ultimately, it will be shown that smart city initiatives and programs akin to it have shown they lead to dependency, not prosperity.

The political polarization America is experiencing is mostly due to the multiple economic crises the country has confronted. The perpetual fraud of banking cartels, combined with the lack of government enforcement of laws that matter, has ultimately put too much stress on the current economic system. The rise in political populism and nationalism is a consequence of this situation; these movements have reached a crescendo in the form of Donald Trump's election in 2016 and the "Brexit" movement for Great Britain in Europe.

In recent years for the United States, two states truly personify the wedge between progressives and conservatives and individualists and collectivists. Both California and Colorado lead the way in this regard; each state's political demographics mirror the culture war that America is currently experiencing. California

20

has always been considered a political bellwether for the country in many areas. As its populous cities lead the way in progressive and socialist politics, the outlying areas that tend to be more conservative feel more disconcerted with the state's direction. In Colorado, Denver and Boulder's proclaimed sanctuary-city status served as a catalyst for statewide discussion on these issues and was ultimately the result of a socialist revolution. Districts that were once considered conservative hotbeds are now political battlegrounds or voting democratic across the board. Why is this relevant to discussing what defines and maintains the idea of the "American Dream?" California's progressive political infrastructure has led the nation when it comes to the implementation of sustainable development programs. It has also helped lead other states like Colorado, to create political change seemingly overnight. Political scientists have even labeled Colorado's political revolution as "The Colorado Method." The ideas implemented in California and Colorado will continue to be utilized by politicians in other cities and states.

Overall, the theories promoted by progressive politicians are directly related to the implementation of a new technocratic political order that poses a direct threat to what previous generations in America defined as "The American Dream." The ability to own a home, save financially, have children, and the ability to retire are all under threat from this new type of system. California's sizeable homeless population evidences this reality with income inequality remaining unchanged no matter what plan progressive leaders put forward. Many states and their towns are taking on new political refugees, as more people flee California's unsustainable market. It seems as if the process is repeating itself in Colorado and elsewhere. Both states have had recent secession movements that illustrate the political dichotomy America is currently faced with. More importantly, both states personify the current ideological battle between political individualists and collectivists. Although the implementation of sustainable development and socialist programs may seem localized now, it is coming to a town near you if it isn't already present.

As these new economic and technological plans manifest themselves, it will become evident that the proposals offered by the supporters of sustainable development and the United Nations' Agenda 2030 are in direct conflict with America's Constitutional legal definition of property rights and human rights. Americans are sacrificing what is sacred only to satisfy their need for more convenience. The current social trend for technological efficiency and comfort is redefining the "American Dream" and what it means to be part of the middle class. Furthermore, American institutions are again making the mistake of allowing the political elite to hold most of the property. What kind of implications does this have for human rights? We must ponder what our Founding Fathers would say about our current economic system as it relates to our national ideals. We must not forget the notion that property rights are synonymous with human rights. Otherwise, the American Dream will transform into an American technocratic nightmare.

Of course, it would be futile to present all of the clear and present dangers to homeownership and middle class living without offering solutions. After objectively examining some of the problems America currently faces, we will also present remedies based on the original ideals that helped America create the largest middle class in the history of the world. Overall, these ideals are built on grassroots innovation and individual liberty as opposed to more regulation from the heavy hand of government.

II
A Short History of Property Rights in America

"Get off my lawn."
Clint Eastwood in "Gran Torino"

Since the dawn of man, philosophers like Plato and Socrates have debated what constitutes free will. Generally, the conversations they had mainly focused on the constant ideological battles between individualism and collectivism. This debate forges its way through matters concerning economics, politics, and sociology. Among the multiple topics they discussed, one of the most critical questions they sought to answer is whether natural law allows an individual to hold title to physical property. In the end, the answer will develop a conclusive political ideology towards economics and individual human rights. Does a human have the right to possess the fruits of their labor? This question has inspired communists, socialists, and capitalists alike, whether it be Karl Marx, Friedrich Engels, and Jean-Jacques Rousseau or Adam Smith and John Locke. They all posited their theories on economics and human rights during the 18th and 19th centuries. We must examine their ideas and determine why it is undeniable that individuals should own title to their labor and the fruits generated from it. America's Founding Fathers believed in individual freedom to make different choices within the local market. After our discourse is complete, it will become clear that the maintenance of individual rights must include some sort of access to physical property where equity can be earned and where freedom of choice is respected. Although all political ideologies acknowledge these functions in part, there is only one ideology that respects them in full. It is undeniable that classical liberalism has promoted individual property ownership more than any other political philosophy.

The ideological battle begins when philosophers determine the source of man's consciousness and their "self," and how that determination directly relates to deciding the origin of someone's individual liberties. Ancient philosophers began this inquiry by determining the true source of mankind. Man's creator could be represented as a God, many gods, a non-existent god, a system

23

of order, or chaos. Overall, this system represents the nature of all things in the world and the universe. The Greeks perceived this system as gods or deities with specifically assigned powers. They saw the universe as observed, the nature of the planets, the sun, the moon, the atmosphere, the water, and the animal kingdom. Even though they did not have access to the scientific knowledge developed in the post-enlightenment era, they did comprehend some sort of system existed. The multiple philosophical debates that occurred built a strong foundation for creating a cohesive definition for the natural laws of survival man must adhere to in order to exist.

But what about the natural state of man? Philosophers tend to agree in some form with Plato's words in *The Republic* that "there is a faculty residing in the soul of each person, and an instrument enabling each of us to learn...."[1] It is that instrument which illuminates our mind's natural ability to think for ourselves, what most philosophers define as "free will." The ancients argued that this ability to choose is an innate characteristic of man when he is in a complete state of nature. What one does with that free will, and how it relates to others, is where philosophers begin to differentiate themselves from each other. What is the source of this free will? Should it remain in an uninhibited, natural state, or should it be restrained? When discussing mankind's relationship with natural law, it is then that individual political theories are born.

The Collectivist Perspective

Communists and socialists alike also believe one's surrounding natural environment develops human consciousness. Communist philosopher Karl Marx states: "Life is not determined by consciousness, but consciousness by life."[2] In other words, Marx believes human consciousness is derived from natural law. Undeniably, Marx's philosophical perspective is built upon his interpretation of natural law, much of which is based on the ancient theories that preceded him. He does not deny that free-will or hu-

[1] Plato, "The Republic" in *Classics of Political & Moral Philosophy*, ed. Steven M. Cahn, 2012, p.131)

[2] Karl M. Marx and Friedrich M. Engels, "The German Ideology," in *Classics of Political & Moral Philosophy*, ed. Steven M. Cahn (New York, NY: Oxford University Press, 2012), p.873)

man consciousness exists.

In addition to consciousness being dependent upon nature, Marx contends that free will also rely on one's social environment. Marx argued that human consciousness could not exist without input from other humans. In Karl Marx and Friedrich Engels' *The German Ideology*, they say that "Consciousness is…a social product, and remains so as long as men exist at all."[3] Although they recognize the individual, they argue that others' collective input is more important or more influential. When he refers to human consciousness as a social product, he refers to a social outcome observed by the individual, which results in an individual outcome.

If individual consciousness is dependent on the community's societal input, personal economic choices are also presumably dependent on the will of the collective society. Marx's philosophical theories on man's natural state and how it is dependent on the collective group directly mirrors his interpretation of economics. Communists contend that an individual's perceived self-worth is solely based on one's production related to the community. Whether in a capitalist society or communist society,

> What they are, therefore, coincides with their production, both with what they produce and with *how* they produce. The nature of individuals thus depends on the material conditions determining their production.[4]

Marx and communist thinkers alike perceive the human consciousness as a consequence of societal input and economic outcomes. They argue a person's free will is always bound to the community's economic production and the environmental and social effects attached to it. Overall, they see the individual's value based on the resources one can contribute to the group, from a top-down perspective.

Marx argued that the individual only served at the top of the social hierarchy during the early stages of mankind when survival was paramount and where a hunter-gatherer mentality was most prominent. As man continued to develop and engage with one another, communities were created, and the social dynamic changed forever. Now, anything that is viewed from an individual perspective must be disregarded, as self-interest ultimately leads

[3] Ibid. 874.

[4] Ibid. 870.

to inequality, which could destroy the collective group's rights and privileges.

The leftist political philosophy promotes the theory that individuals acting in a competitive environment will always lead to mass inequality. Competition is derived from an individual's uninhibited free will, or as Marx puts it, their "material behavior."[5] Jean-Jacques Rousseau contends in his *Discourse on the Origin of Inequality* that:

> From the moment one man began to require the help of another; from the moment it appeared advantageous to any one man to have enough provisions for two, equality disappeared, property was introduced...and where slavery and misery were soon seen to germinate and grow up with the crops.[6]

Without a doubt, Rousseau is attacking free-market ideology by attaching capitalism and property rights to slavery, inequality, and misery. Similarly, in Karl Marx's *Economic and Philosophic Manuscripts of 1844*, he proclaims that the result of free-market competition is the accumulation of wealth in a few hands where society is divided into two classes: property *owners* and property-less *workers*.[7] Undoubtedly, Marx and Rousseau share similar beliefs towards the relationship between property accumulation and the human condition.

In Marx's mind, for human rights to be upheld, the concept of the "material self" must be replaced with the "common good." By doing so, citizens can create a society free of inequality where people can reach their individual potential. By respecting the will of the common good, individuals can maximize their own free will. Otherwise, a person will sacrifice their self-expression by succumbing to the market's violent and irrational chaos. Marx states:

> Man makes his life activity itself the object of his will and of his consciousness...it is only because he is a species being that he is a conscious being, i.e., that his own life is an object for him. Only because of that is his activity free activity. Estranged labor reverses this relationship, so that it is just be-

5 Ibid. 870.

6 Jean-Jacques Rousseau, "Discourse on the Origin of Inequality," in *Classics of Political & Moral Philosophy*, ed. Steven M. Cahn (New York: Oxford University Press, 2012), p.557)

7 Karl Marx and Friedrich Engels, "The German Ideology," in *Classics of Political & Moral Philosophy*, ed. Steven M. Cahn (New York: Oxford University Press, 2012), p.862)

cause man is a conscious being that he makes his life activity, his *essential* being, a mere means to his *existence.*[8]

Marx accurately illustrates his view that unfettered competition in the market results in fruitless labor, which forces the individual to supply work that is dependent on current economic conditions, rather than them providing labor based on a person's innate drive towards self-expression. Only when an individual's contributions to society are based on the common good where labor and resources are shared collectively, can one realize their dreams.

Of course, unregulated self-expression results in the "mine, mine, mine" mentality among individuals, according to Marx, Hegel, Rousseau, and others like them. It is a paradoxical argument; on the one hand, Marx contends that for an individual to reach their full potential, they must collectively share their resources, yet if that full potential is reached, Marx cynically focuses on man's ego, which will always want more. How can the system continue? Ultimately, the concept of the individual must be destroyed. For this to happen, individual private ownership must cease to exist. Marx states: "wages are a direct consequence of estranged labor, and estranged labor is the direct cause of private property. The downfall of the one must involve the downfall of the other."[9] It is at this point in Marx's argument, where his intentions become clear. Marx believes that a balance must be struck between individual and collective rights where the state, i.e., the people, has full control over society's market functions to ensure equality for all citizens. Wages must be distributed equally among the populace. For this to occur, the concept of private property must be eliminated. The ideology is fully outlined in Marx's *Manifesto of the Communist Party*[10]:

1. Abolition of property in land and application of all rents of land to public purposes.
2. A heavy progressive or graduated income tax.
3. Abolition of all right of inheritance.
4. Confiscation of the property of all emigrants and rebels.
5. Centralization of credit in the hands of the state, by means of a national bank with state capital and an exclu-

---

[8] Ibid. 865.

[9] Ibid. 868.

[10] Karl Marx and Friedrich Engels, "Manifesto of the Communist Party," in *Classics of Political & Moral Philosophy*, ed. Steven M. Cahn (New York: Oxford University Press, 2012), p.889)

sive monopoly.

6. Centralization of the means of communication and transport in the hands of the state.

7. Extension of factories and instruments of production owned by the state; the bringing into cultivation of wastelands, and the improvement of soil generally in accordance with a common plan.

8. Equal liability of all to labor. Establishment of industrial armies, especially for agriculture.

9. Combination of agriculture with manufacturing industries; gradual abolition of the distinction between town and country, by a more equable distribution of the population over the country.

10. Free education for all children in public schools. Abolition of children's factory labor in its present form. Combination of education with industrial production, etc.

In the end, Marx argues that "in the course of development, class distinctions have disappeared…the public power will lose its political character…political power…is merely the organized power of one class for oppressing another."[11] Marx believes that unregulated competition in the market leads to a selfish form of self-expression, which inevitably leads to inequality throughout the community. His theories advocate equitable regulation of competition and its close relative, individual liberty. Through and through, it is undeniable that those on the left end of the political spectrum argue that personal freedom can only be maintained if property rights are entirely abolished. Ultimately, communists and socialists believe that property rights have consistently been used throughout history to form two classes: the oppressors (property owners) and those oppressed (laborers.)

The Classical Liberal/Libertarian Perspective

While political collectivists like Marx and Rousseau promote natural rights as a healthy relationship between individual liberty and the group's general welfare, it is evident that after dissecting their writings, they believe that the community's welfare as a whole outweighs the rights of the individuals that compose it. They contend that self-expression should be restricted as man's

[11] Ibid. 889.

natural state will throw the world's natural order into chaos. The idea of the sovereign individual and individual property ownership must be eliminated.

In blatant contrast, libertarian philosophers have a different interpretation of human consciousness's origins and the individual rights born from it. In their minds, an individual's self-identity depends on their ability to fully express themselves according to natural law. They contend that individual expression is born of man's consciousness, which exists in man's natural state. For this reason, they believe man's free will should be celebrated as being a part of nature, not a separate consequence of it. They argue that the source of "self" and consciousness is beholden to individuals with different traits based on natural law. In their view, it is normal for humans to focus on self-preservation, a feature that should be celebrated and considered as part of the natural order of all things.

As long as an individual does not injure another's ability to live free, they can express themselves without consequence. Furthermore, civil libertarians contend that society directly benefits from their creations when humans are allowed to express themselves. They also believe that the source of "self" and consciousness is beholden to individuals with different individual rights sourced from nature or God. These ideas strongly differ from the communist and socialist concepts of the same era, where the community's collective will is considered synonymous with the natural order of all things, outweighing the individual's aspirations and ego. Classical liberals argue that individual free will represents the proper natural order where all economic and political theories can derive its meaning. John Locke is widely known as an important philosopher among classical liberals. The original political definition of liberalism mainly focused on individual liberty and equal rights. Locke and others have posited that government's primary function is to protect life, liberty, and property. Since then, that definition has transformed into serving equal outcomes, which is different. Rousseau's interpretation of Locke's writings was the beginning of many variations that have subtly changed this concept. Instead of focusing on material outcomes, Locke focuses on equal opportunity. Instead of focusing on the idea of the self as being a consequence of nature, he sees man as being part of nature with individual free will, unlike its animal counterparts. Ultimately, Locke considers the source of individual liberty as an intrinsic part of the natural order of things in a symbiotic relationship with natural law. In other words, an individual's rights come from nature or God. In his view, the individual's ability to choose must be respected to maintain harmony with nature.

In Locke's *Second Treatise of Government*, the definition of classical liberalism is illustrated beautifully by outlining his key definitions regarding natural law, man's relation to it, the rights that are formed from it, and the government that interprets and enforces it. He begins by formulating his ideas on man's natural state, demonstrating how consciousness and political power are central to it:

> To understand political power, right, and derive it from its original, we must consider what state all men are naturally in, and that is, *a state of perfect freedom* to order their actions, as they think fit, within the bounds of the law of nature; without asking leave, or depending upon the will of any other man.[12]

It is incontrovertible that Locke's assertion argues that man is independent of the group it belongs to, as man is always in a state of perfect freedom.

The sovereign man will serve in a community that is sovereign to its larger counterpart, if any. Both operate as sovereign entities that function with each other's consent. Locke highlights these sentiments in his "social contract." Overall, he stipulates that since man is in a constant state of nature, independent and free on its own, man must consent to enter into a contract with civil society:

> Man being born, as has been proved, with a title to perfect freedom, and an uncontrolled enjoyment of all the rights and privileges of the law of nature, equally with any other man, or number of men in the world, hath by nature a power, not only to preserve property, that is, his life, liberty, and estate, against injuries and attempts of other men…in crimes where the heinousness of the fact, in his opinion, requires it.[13]

This society can write its laws to protect individual liberty by ensuring no individuals or groups injure one another:

> And thus the commonwealth comes by a power to set down what punishment shall belong to the several transgressions

[12] John Locke, "Second Treatise of Government," in *Classics of Political & Moral Philosophy*, ed. Steven M. Cahn (New York: Oxford University Press, 2012), p.451)

[13] Ibid. 472.

which they think worthy of it, committed amongst the members of that society…as well as it has the power to punish any injury done unto any of its members, by anyone that is not of it, and all this for the preservation of the property of all the members of that society, as far as possible.[14]

It is observable that Locke sees the individual as atoms in a larger structure, each living independently of one another, with the ability to enter into contracts with other individuals and larger groups voluntarily. Of course, these contracts must be based on natural law, or civil liberties will be sacrificed.

Undeniably, humans can only survive by laboring for their specific needs. Locke argues that the ability to work and hold ownership to the rewards from that labor is part of man's natural rights. He continues to theorize that if this labor involves property, a man should hold exclusive rights to it:

The law man was under, was rather for appropriating. God commanded, and his wants forced him to *labour*. That was his *property* which could not be taken from him wherever he had fixed it. And hence subduing or cultivating the earth, and having dominion, we see are joined together. So that God, by commanding to subdue, gave authority so far to appropriate, and the condition of human life, which requires labor and materials to work on, necessarily introduces private possessions.[15]

Laboring for one's sustenance is undoubtedly a form of self-expression. If a man cannot hold title to his self-expression, his rights are limited, and this would ultimately result in a collapse in economic productivity. This outcome is the result of denying the natural laws of self-preservation, which is inherent to all living things. In other words, Locke believes that private property does not belong to others unless provided by mutual consent. Locke shapes his argument as such:

…yet man, by being master of himself, and *proprietor of his own person, and the actions or labour of it, had still in himself the great foundation of property;* and that, which made up the great part of what he applied to the support or comfort of his being, when invention and arts had improved the con-

14 Ibid. 473.

15 Ibid. 459.

venience of life, was perfectly his own, and did not belong in common to others.[16]

In summary, it is self-evident that Locke believed an individual's natural rights are directly dependent on one's ability to create and generate sustenance. Furthermore, he contends that the human condition can only be improved if individuals have a direct stake in the labor they exhaust for their survival.

The argument for sustained individual self-expression is not merely a spiritual or philosophical one. Classical thinkers like Adam Smith have put forth economic motivations as well. Their opinions bridge the gap between an individual's self-expression and the fundamental economic laws common in all markets.

Overall, Smith argues that when individuals are allowed to choose what type of labor suits their interests, the division of labor throughout the economy becomes more efficient and sustainable. In this way, Smith is celebrating individuality as a specific utility within the market. He elaborates on this fact in *The Wealth of Nations*:

> The difference of natural talents in different men is, in reality, much less than we are aware of; and the very different genius which appears to distinguish men of different professions…is not upon many occasions so much the cause, as the effect of the division of labor.[17]

He argues that a non-centric market built on multiple forms of labor allows individuals to create and invent in an environment where they do not have to focus on facilitating every human need. If another member of society is growing food, they do not necessarily need to grow food. If another member of the community herds livestock, they do not have to focus on herding livestock. Smith breaks down the structure of labor from an individual perspective:

> When the division of labour has been…established, it is but a very small part of a man's wants which the produce of his own labour can supply. He supplies the far greater part of them by exchanging that surplus part of the produce of his own labour, which is over and above his own consumption… Every man thus lives by exchanging, or becomes in some

<hr>

[16] Ibid. 462.

[17] Adam Smith, "The Wealth of Nations," in *Classics of Political & Moral Philosophy*, ed. Steven M. Cahn (New York: Oxford University Press, 2012), p.668)

measure a merchant, and the society itself grows to be what is properly a commercial society.[18]

Smith paints an accurate picture of the fundamental forces within the market. Allowing individuals to provide labor based on their own interests will enable individuals to ascertain the benefits of trading and exchange for other needs. In other words, people have more time to focus on their craft, which undeniably creates more professionals and experts.

By combining the arguments of John Locke and Adam Smith, it becomes self-evident that individuals have natural, unalienable rights. These rights are based on natural law, who can only realize their potential through self-expression in a free market environment.

When comparing both philosophical arguments, it is obvious that Locke's theories are soundly based on natural law. All classical philosophers helped build this definition, although they differ in many ways. However, Locke's arguments on what constitutes consciousness and "self" seem to be based in reality, while others prove unequivocally idealistic. Although Karl Marx and Jean-Jacques Rousseau would like to believe you can accurately suppress an individual's will to support the greater good, it is impossible as it ultimately ignores natural law. Locke accurately illustrated this point by arguing self-preservation is a form of self-ownership for an individual; if you deny the property generated from a person's labor, you deny the rights he or she was born with. This environment ultimately leads to apathy among members of society. Without a doubt, both Locke and Smith prove that the individual's success eventually leads to the group's success. These resolutions helped define modern definitions of property rights. Through and through, communist and socialist thinkers deny what constitutes our very existence as humans and the natural laws that our liberties are based on.

The Constitutional Perspective

Without a doubt, the ideas of John Locke and Adam Smith had a substantial impact on the Founding Fathers of the United States. John Locke's ideas were integral to the Declaration of Independence's issuance, and Smith's *The Wealth of Nations*

[18] Ibid. 669.

was published in the pivotal year of 1776. Both men significantly influenced the academics of their time. Classical liberalism helped define what constitutes the individual, the consciousness within that individual, and the natural laws that the individual must subscribe to. Property rights are based on natural law, and natural law helped craft our founding documents. You can see how vital this relationship is by examining ancient philosophical discussions and how they were integral to Western civilization's formation as we know it today. Consider the infamous line within the Declaration of Independence:

> We hold these truths to be self-evident, that all men are created equal, that they are endowed by their Creator with certain unalienable Rights, that among these are Life, Liberty, and the pursuit of Happiness.

Unmistakably, it is clear the Founding Fathers derived their ideas from classical liberalism. Locke consistently refers to the statement "Life, Liberty, and Estate Property" throughout his opinions. Many had questioned Thomas Jefferson's choice to replace "property" with "pursuit of Happiness" in the Declaration. Arguably, the pursuit itself relies on individual self-expression; when considering Locke's arguments, this line still implies that property ownership is integral to the American Dream. Although some may clamor for a more defined term, the broad wording of "pursuit of Happiness" effectively calls on the will of the human spirit to realize its full potential.

Most historians agree that property rights formed the basis for the Declaration of Independence and the United States Constitution that followed it. Edmund S. Morgan puts it best:

> For eighteenth-century Americans, property and liberty were one and inseparable, because property was the only foundation yet conceived for security of life and liberty: without security for his property, it was thought, no man could live or be free except at the mercy of another.[19]

Lockean theory undoubtedly supports this thesis. Locke accurately depicted that securing life was only possible by obtaining property through one's labor.

The entire Declaration is an indictment against England

---

[19] Edmund S. Morgan, "The American Revolution: Revisions in Need of Revising," William & Mary Quarterly, 3rd series, 14, no. 1 (1957), p. 11.

for denying the colonists' human rights with rampant taxation and a concerted attack on their sovereignty as individuals and as a nation. They alleged that England was denying their unalienable rights like taxing them without their consent, depriving them of trial by jury, or suspending their local legislatures. When examining these issues individually, it is clear that England's injuries against the American colonists denied the core utilities of natural law. Even Rousseau and Marx reject the premise of kings' divine right, which directly conflicts with the concept of natural rights. Locke simply recognized that the protection of the individual was the only route to glorify what constitutes natural law.

The U.S. Constitution helped craft a system the founders believed would prevent future usurpations. They aimed to form a government that protected life, liberty, and property. Overall, the founding documents help create a strong foundation for creating a sustainable society and government. By recognizing the sovereign individual first, citizens can build a government that suits their needs. Political leaders derive their power from the individuals they represent. The three branches of government outlined in the Constitution are sovereign and independent from each other. On the world stage, the United States' Declaration also recognizes the empowered legislature and the states they represent as a sovereign nation. Overall, t his entire structure is based on Locke's arguments concerning natural law.

When examining the United States Constitution, one can derive a connection to property ownership throughout the document. We will discuss some of the key clauses as well as the Bill of Rights. By providing examples with each clause, it will become self-evident that property rights embody all of our unalienable rights in some way or another.[20]

Bill of Rights

I.   **Congress shall make no law respecting an establishment of religion, or prohibiting the free exercise thereof; or abridging the freedom of speech, or of the press; or the right of the people peaceably to assemble, and to petition the Government for a redress of grievances.**

[20] United States Constitution. 1787.

Of course, for freedom of the press to exist, you need printing presses and writers. Writers need an office to work out of. Would one expect the news media to be impartial if they were forced to work out of a government-owned office with government oversight? Would Churches be allowed to impartially practice their religion if governments were allowed to regulate or own them?

II.   A well regulated Militia, being necessary to the security of a free State, the right of the people to keep and bear Arms, shall not be infringed.

By dissecting the wording of this amendment, we are answering two questions. How does this amendment relate to property rights? And does this amendment preserve individual gun ownership rights? As confirmed by Antonin Scalia's majority opinion in the case of Columbia v. Heller, "the right of the people to keep and bear arms" is a separate part of the overall sentence structure, with a point of emphasis added with a comma at the end. Scalia states that the amendment could be rephrased to: "Because a well regulated Militia is necessary to the security of a free State, the right of the people to keep and bear Arms shall not be infringed."[21] These arguments were grounded in the concept of self-preservation, which is undeniably built upon Locke's ideas concerning natural law. The term "bear" is possessive of "arms," signaling ownership to physical property.

III.   No Soldier shall, in time of peace be quartered in any house, without the consent of the Owner, nor in time of war, but in a manner to be prescribed by law.

This amendment was established in response to England forcing American colonists to house British soldiers. The colonists viewed this as a direct violation of their individual sovereignty. The house is man's domain, his kingdom, if you will. It is tyrannical to violate people's space without probable cause.

IV.   The right of the people to be secure in their

[21] DISTRICT OF COLUMBIA et al. v. HELLER, 554 U.S. Report 570 (June 26, 2008).

persons, houses, papers, and effects, against unreasonable searches and seizures, shall not be violated, and no Warrants shall issue, but upon probable cause, supported by Oath or affirmation, and particularly describing the place to be searched, and the persons or things to be seized.

The fourth amendment is very similar to the third regarding property rights, however much more explicit. It covers *all* forms of individual property ownership. Overall, this amendment protects people's property by requiring certification of probable cause (a warrant) to enter someone's house, search them physically, or seize property.

V.   **No person shall be held to answer for a capital, or otherwise infamous crime, unless on a presentment or indictment of a Grand Jury, except in cases arising in the land or naval forces, or in the Militia, when in actual service in time of War or public danger; nor shall any person be subject for the same offence to be twice put in jeopardy of life or limb; nor shall any person be subject for the same offence to be twice put in jeopardy of life or limb; nor shall be compelled in any criminal case to be a witness against himself, nor be deprived of life, liberty, or property, without due process of law; nor shall private property be taken for public use, without just compensation.**

Much of this amendment relates to criminal prosecution. Concerning property rights, it mandates that man cannot be deprived of life, liberty, or property, without due process. The concept of eminent domain immediately comes to mind, where governments can seize property for public use. The amendment specifically requires "just compensation."

VI.   **In all criminal prosecutions, the accused shall enjoy the right to a speedy and public trial, by an impartial jury of the State and district where-**

in the crime shall have been committed, which district shall have been previously ascertained by law, and to be informed of the nature and cause of the accusation; to be confronted with the witnesses against him; to have compulsory process for obtaining witnesses in his favor, and to have the assistance of counsel for his defence.

The sixth amendment relates to criminal prosecutions again; however, there is a subtle reference to property appropriation. "By an impartial jury of the State and district wherein the crime shall have been committed" indicates a specific location. The surrounding property is maintained by local residents, indicating that the injury to the people and their property must be represented in the court procedure. This amendment also relates to providing due process for the accused, where the loss of liberty and property is at stake.

VII.   **In Suits at common law, where the value in controversy shall exceed twenty dollars, the right of trial by jury shall be preserved, and no fact tried by a jury, shall be otherwise re-examined in any Court of the United States, than according to the rules of the common law.**

Civil suits typically deal directly with property, and the administration of property is based on common law. The seventh amendment is vital for protecting property rights as it requires a jury trial for suits involving large sums of capital. The parties involved could be "the people" versus an individual or individuals, or two individuals versus each other.

VIII.   **Excessive bail shall not be required, nor excessive fines imposed, nor cruel and unusual punishments inflicted.**

If excessive bail was assessed on the most trivial types of criminal cases, it could destroy someone's life. In doing so, the state would be arbitrarily seizing individual property. In other words, the punishment must be deemed as equitable to the crime.

IX.   The enumeration in the Constitution, of certain rights, shall not be construed to deny or disparage others retained by the people.

The founders were concerned that if there were an outlined "Bill of Rights" in the Constitution, other rights that were not explicitly listed would be ignored. These rights would be defined through the courts and interpretation of common law. With the ninth amendment, these rights must be respected as well.

X.   The powers not delegated to the United States by the Constitution, nor prohibited by it to the States, are reserved to the States respectively, or to the people.

In other words, when examining a particular issue, if the Constitution does not list a specific power to the federal Congress, it is reserved for the individual states that compose the federal government. Today, marijuana legalization in certain states has challenged Congress' recently created the Drug Enforcement Agency and their classification of drugs. Many legal scholars question the premise that the Federal government can regulate substances they deem illegal. State-by-state legalization has allowed the creation of private marijuana dispensary businesses, in conflict with current Federal law. Legalization advocates argue that since the Federal government does not have this power delegated to them, it is reserved to the states. In this case, the 10th amendment is effectively protecting the private property of marijuana dispensary owners and consumers.

The American "Bundle of Rights"

Without a doubt, America's founding in 1776 marked a sharp turn in humanity's definition of individual property rights. Although many historians look upon America's westward expansion as an affront to the rights and condition of the native peoples, it did allow for a new understanding of how individuals occupy the land and the rights provided therein. The simple irony is that even America, in its early beginnings, violated its current definition of individual property rights. This type of hypocrisy is nothing new—as you will see, America's history and human history, in general, are defined by how property rights are interpreted and subsequently enforced. Ultimately, this comprehensive definition represents a constant battle on an ever-changing spectrum of political philosophy. This definition is built upon years of legal precedence; to fully understand today's interpretation of property rights, we must understand the foundation it was originally built upon.

In the early days of America's westward expansion, pioneers that headed west claimed ownership to land by merely marking it with some kind of natural marker, like a stick, or a flag and eventually a fence or barrier. This was different from man's early days, when humans lived with a hunter-gatherer mentality, following a nomadic path for food and water. It was not until man began to cultivate land that property ownership became important. This eventually developed into Europe's feudal systems where groups gathered, and heads of state or "kings" were given divine right over land and the responsibility to maintain it for the people. The kings' "subjects" were given small tracts of land to maintain under the Kings' supervision. Europe's collectivized version of property rights led to institutionalized oppression and mass starvation, which helped spark multiple revolutions across Europe, culminating with the French Revolution in 1789. Across the water, the Americans were also revolting against their colonial oppressors.

Europe's feudalistic land allocation was replaced with an allodial system where individuals were given the right to own land. At first, the feudal lords became owners, and the peasants remained tenants of the lords. Then, the peasants eventually became owners as well. This is the critical difference between the two systems—one allows for economic mobility, and the other does not. Economic mobility is the difference between a stable state and an unstable one prone to revolution from its people. These ideas were eventually expanded upon; once man realized that he was no longer a subject, but an owner, he realized that he was an individual first. Why should we answer to a government that resides 3000 miles away across an ocean? Why should we pay taxes to a government that does not uphold the rights and will of the people? These questions were answered with America's revolution in 1776.

The American system of property allocation expanded further on Europe's comprehension of individual property rights. In Europe, there tends to be more considerable interest in public ownership of land versus private. Although Europeans can own land, they have chosen to fund broader government ownership of land, which comes with inherent political power. There is no such thing as the 2nd Amendment or "king of the castle" laws in Europe, and if they do exist, they are primarily watered down. The allodial system of land allocation provides individuals with a "bundle of rights." They are labeled as a "bundle of rights" because, at one time, before proper record keeping, this bundle was a literal bundle of physical emblements that represented different rights. Europeans have simply chosen to allocate more rights for the government than their American counterparts. In the American real estate language, *Fee Simple Ownership* is the largest, most complete bundle of rights one can hold in land. The Fee Simple Bundle of Rights contains:

- Occupy and Use
- Build
- Grant Easements
- Mortgage
- Mine, Drill, Farm
- Restrict Use
- Covenant
- Exclude Others
- Sell
- Refuse to Sell
- Give Away, Abandon
- Rent or Lease
- License
- Devise by Will

As you can see, the list is expansive. Any infringement on these individual rights, or voluntary exemption, is defined as an *encumbrance.*

Encumbrances are defined as any claim, right, lien, estate, or liability that limits the fee simple title to property. *Title* is defined as the right to or ownership of something, also the evidence of ownership, such as a deed or bill of sale. This term is vitally important to understand how we can lose our property rights and individual rights. Sometimes we voluntarily give up these rights; the most common example of this is the landlord-tenant relationship. A landlord willingly gives up his right to occupy and use his property so that his/her tenant can do so. Likewise, a tenant does not have the right to sell his landlord's property. To expand on this further, if we provide consent to the government to tax our property (tax lien, anybody?), that consent comes with a contract. In this case, that contract is based on the government's ability to make decisions *with our permission.* Equally important is the government's ability to enforce these types of arrangements. Most would contend this is the government's most vital function.

It is self-evident that individual rights are property rights, and it is undeniable that one cannot exist without the other. These legal definitions have been built upon hundreds of years of historical precedence, which most scholars define as common law. We have examined early political philosophers' writings and have determined that property rights are intertwined with the definition of individual rights no matter the political perspective. We have discovered that the definition of individual rights tends to fall within two political spectrums: one that is defined as being classically liberal and individualistic, and one that is defined as being collectivist, or Marxist, in nature. Property rights are not exempt; the systems fall in line with either a feudalistic system that is collectivist in function or the allodial system that upholds classical liberalism's core tenets. History has shown us that feudalistic systems have led to mass oppression and starvation, resulting in multiple revolutions across the world, which resulted in America's revolution and the creation of the U.S. Constitution. The next question to ask is, what modern political theories represent the most significant threat, or "encumbrance" to the allodial allocation of property rights, individual rights, and the U.S. Constitution that was designed to protect them?

III

The Rise of 3,000 Kings

"Why would I trade one tyrant 3000 miles away for 3000 tyrants
one mile away?"
Mather Byles, Boston Loyalist, 1775

The precautionary principle is a theory that was born
out of the environmental movement during the early 1960s and
1970s by political scientists and environmentalists. Books like
Rachel's Carson's *Silent Spring,* which focused on harmful
pesticides and herbicides, argued the theory that these chemicals
could eventually lead to cancers in humans and animals. It holds
that as humans, there are consequences to our actions that may
be unknown to us at present. In their view, every action made
throughout our daily lives has potential consequences. It is our
job to help understand or hypothesize what is possible and prevent any adverse outcomes. There are consequences that we are
aware of, such as obvious oil pollution in our oceans and rivers
or the carbon monoxide poisoning in our air. There are also
some outcomes that we are unaware of, such as cancer from the
asbestos used in general construction during the mid 20th century,
which could only be determined at a much later time through
the course of many studies, and people merely getting sick! The
National Institute of Health states that the precautionary principle
has four central components:

- taking preventive action in the face of uncertainty;
- shifting the burden of proof to the proponents of an activity;
- exploring a wide range of alternatives to possibly harmful actions;
- and increasing public participation in decision making.[1]

The ability to predict the future has always been a keen

---

[1] D. Kriebel et al., "The Precautionary Principle in Environmental Science," Environmental Health
Perspectives, September 2001, accessed August 18, 2020, https://www.ncbi.nlm.nih.gov/pmc/articles/
PMC1240435/)

interest of mankind, however impossible it may be. This narrative's primary goal is to prove that the precautionary principle is intrinsically flawed due to its blatant disregard for the scientific method and human nature in general. Most scholars would agree that the scientific method is utilized throughout all areas of study, whether it be biology, astronomy, history, or math. Concrete evidence must be provided, and trustworthy sources must be cited for arguments to be considered valid. Overall, we will find that the interpretation and enforcement of the precautionary principle do neither. Secondarily, it will be shown that the precautionary principle has intertwined itself into all types of government policy, whether it be environmental policy, foreign policy, or economic policy. By continually searching for government solutions to problems that are either: a) out of mankind's control or b) no problems at all, the government finds itself enforcing policies that promote common burdens rather than the common good. Finally, we will show that the precautionary principle has been utilized to justify the exponential growth of government in America, inevitably destroying our founding principles in the process.

Our ignorance as humans will always complicate the process of delegating errors and successes to specific actions. Although some believe otherwise, humans are not perfect and never will be. Of course, we must make attempts to improve the human condition; this is admirable and necessary. However, other aspects of human life simply cannot be regulated or controlled; there will always be outcomes that remain unpredictable. As the saying goes, "life is never fair or perfect."

Everyone has an opinion on the role of government. Some believe it needs to be as small as possible; some believe it needs to be expansive with committees devoted to certain areas of expertise with strong regulatory power. Have Americans become addicted to government intervention in every aspect of their lives? Without a doubt, the size of government has expanded drastically in the last fifty years or so. One could easily argue that this is due to the devotion to concepts like the precautionary principle. The precautionary principle is a direct result of the continuation of ideas from both sides of the political spectrum, led by neoliberals and neoconservatives alike. Yes, the theory earned recognition at the onset of the environmental movement. However, the argument is the same for the entire political spectrum; certain actions or behavior that are detrimental to humanity or society in some way must be mitigated, controlled, or removed entirely. No matter the concern, the recommended response is always some form of government intervention from a panel of "specialists."

The precautionary principle has spread like wildfire throughout all walks of life and is not relegated to issues surrounding the natural environment. Over time, society has become accustomed to the notion that perceived problems can always be prevented by regulating and dictating human affairs. When a problem pops up, some type of bureaucracy or group can create a regulation to mitigate or prevent the problem. If that bureaucracy does not exist, American politicians simply create one. In many cases, this type of reaction can be viewed as logical and practical. However, one must ask, where does it end? More importantly, how does it impact our quality of life on this planet?

Without a doubt, most people would agree that human life can be looked at as controlled chaos. Problems occur, and they always will. It would be great to imagine a world where there are no car accidents, violent weather, violent people, poverty, inequality, or war. However, is this type of world possible? Some believe that due to the fact that the modern era likely represents the peak of human civilization due to advancements in our technology that it is truly possible to control or mitigate all aspects of life. With this mindset, it would not be a stretch to say that there must be regulation for every problem. Imagine the amount of paper or disk space one would need to account for all the world's problems! Before we examine the plausibility of enforcing the regulations the government has created, let us examine the size and scope of the regulatory framework throughout the United States of America.

Regulations are a unique aspect of America's legal structure. With American criminal law, it is well known that a citizen is presumed to be innocent until proven guilty. Regulations are different from laws in this regard; with regulations, you are guilty until proven innocent. Forget civil tort law, which is based on deciding liability for a specific injury from one group to another---regulations are in place to *prevent* a possible injury between groups (or even non-existent ones!). It will become evident that there are regulations for every aspect of life. For some areas, preventing an injury is wholly possible through the use of a regulatory framework. However, other areas cannot be supervised or managed, as we will see.

To begin, we will examine the structure of America's bureaucratic empire from the top-down. Here is a full list of executive agencies and regulatory departments in the United States government:

Executive Agencies

1. Department of Agriculture
2. Department of Commerce
3. Department of Defense
4. Department of Education
5. Department of Energy
6. Department of Health and Human Services
7. Department of Homeland Security
8. Department of Housing and Urban Development
9. Department of the Interior
10. Department of Justice
11. Department of Labor
12. Department of State
13. Department of Transportation
14. Department of the Treasury
15. Department of Veterans Affairs

Independent Agencies, Founded Through Acts of Congress

1. Broadcasting Board of Governors
2. Central Intelligence Agency
3. Corporation for National and Community Service
4. Environmental Protection Agency
5. Farm Credit Administration
6. Federal Deposit Insurance Corporation
7. Federal Housing Finance Agency
8. Federal Labor Relations Authority
9. General Services Administration
10. Institute of Museum and Library Services

11. National Aeronautics and Space Administration
12. National Archives and Records Administration
13. National Credit Union Administration
14. National Endowment for the Arts
15. National Endowment for the Humanities
16. National Railroad Passenger Corporation
17. National Science Foundation
18. Office of Government Ethics
19. Office of Personnel Management
20. Overseas Private Investment Corporation
21. Peace Corps
22. Pension Benefit Guaranty Corporation
23. Selective Service System
24. Small Business Administration
25. Social Security Administration
26. Tennessee Valley Authority
27. Thrift Savings Plan
28. United States Agency for International Development
29. United States Postal Service
30. United States Trade and Development Agency

Boards, Commissions, and Committees, Founded Through Acts of Congress

1. Advisory Council on Historic Preservation
2. American Battle Monuments Commission
3. Board of Governors of the Federal Reserve System
4. Commodity Futures Trading Commission
5. Consumer Product Safety Commission
6. Equal Employment Opportunity Commission
7. Federal Communications Commission
8. Federal Election Commission
9. Federal Energy Regulatory Commission
10. Federal Laboratory Consortium for Technology Transfer
11. Federal Maritime Commission

47

12. Federal Mine Safety and Health Review Commission
13. Federal Retirement Thrift Investment Board
14. Federal Trade Commission
15. International Boundary and Water Commission
16. Merit Systems Protection Board
17. National Capital Planning Commission
18. National Council on Disability
19. National Indian Gaming Commission
20. National Labor Relations Board
21. National Transportation Safety Board
22. Nuclear Regulatory Commission
23. Nuclear Waste Technical Review Board
24. Occupational Safety and Health Review Commission
25. Postal Regulatory Commission
26. Railroad Retirement Board
27. Securities and Exchange Commission
28. The United States International Trade Commission

These bureaucracies were created over the 242-year existence of the United States of America, but how? Without understanding constitutional law or politics, most Americans, after reading the U.S. Constitution, are likely to ask: "How did these agencies get created in the first place?" After all, there is not a specific line in the Constitution that says "Congress shall regulate and dictate the affairs of all educational facilities throughout the United States," or "Congress shall provide for the maintenance and transport of all mail in the United States," or "Congress shall create a general retirement fund for all American citizens." When this question is posed in political science circles, the conversation is likely to break off into two separate camps: those that translate the Constitution as written, and those that translate the Constitution as a flexible document open to current and modern interpretations. From this perspective, the meaning of the words in the Constitution and their real-time applications have changed over time, and we must adapt our current laws to those current definitions. These two philosophies are bound to clash with each other.

Through and through, this work aims to highlight the intrinsic flaws within the Constitution itself and the argument that "words and meanings change over time." For many, perceiving the Constitution as a "flexible document" is a creative way to eliminate its legal power. Metaphorically speaking, it is akin to an NBA game having the rules changed before the buzzer has rung. How are you supposed to follow the rules if they are constantly changing over time? It is impossible to do so, which may be the point. If the document is continuously interpreted in different ways throughout U.S. history, one could argue that there is no point in following the rules at all. So, how did we get here? What specific lines in the U.S. constitution have allowed our sneaky politicians to pervert the Constitution's true intentions and its counterpart, the Declaration of Independence?

Many scholars have written full books on this subject, so for the sake of time, we will focus on a few of the main culprits in the document that have provided a "blank check" for U.S. politicians to rip the Constitution to shreds, piece by piece resulting in an ever-expansive Federal government. First, we will focus on the sections within the U.S. Constitution that mention the "general welfare" of the people. The term is mentioned immediately at the beginning of the Constitution's primary objective:

> **We the People** of the United States, in Order to form a more perfect Union, establish Justice, insure domestic Tranquility, provide for the common defence, **promote the general Welfare,** and secure the Blessings of Liberty to ourselves and our Posterity, do ordain and establish this Constitution for the United States of America.

It is mentioned again in Section 8, which specifies the powers of the U.S. Congress:

> The Congress shall have Power To lay and collect Taxes, Duties, Imposts and Excises, to pay the Debts and provide for the common Defence and general Welfare of the United States; but all Duties, Imposts and Excises shall be uniform throughout the United States;

When reading these lines, the political analyst is immediately confronted with multiple questions. "Promote the general Welfare," of what? What constitutes the "general Welfare" of the United States? Does the name "United States" encompass its citi-

49

zens or the country as a whole? Define: "Welfare." The founding fathers had specific references in mind. We will then examine the perceived definition of the notorious "commerce clause," which provides certain powers to Congress regarding inter and intrastate commerce.

For most Americans, the year that our country was founded was 1776, and many falsely believe that the Constitution was created simultaneously as the Declaration of Independence. It was not until 11 years later in 1787 that U.S. leaders met at a constitutional convention to debate the power and scope of the proposed federal government. The convention stirred early debate among the nation's two founding fathers, James Madison and Alexander Hamilton, in their infamous Federalist Papers debates, mainly because it posed serious questions to the size and scope of governmental power and influence throughout the country. To understand the specific clauses that have inevitably expanded the United States government's size over time, we must dissect the early debates that framed the Constitution before its institution on September 18th, 1787.

Alexander Hamilton is the greatest defender of what constitutes the Federal government as we know it today: large and robust with thousands of government bureaucrats. Why did he believe in a confederation of states that is subservient to a more powerful Federal government? In essence, Hamilton contended that states that act solely upon their interests will lead to perpetual war, like Europe, and that there must be a mediator or "enforcer" for the states in the Union:

> It has been seen that delinquencies in the members of the Union are its natural and necessary offspring; and that when-ever they happen, the only constitutional remedy is force, and the immediate effect of the use of it, civil war...If there should not be a large army constantly at the disposal of the national government it would either not be able to employ force at all, or...it would amount to a war between different parts of the Confederacy concerning the infractions of a league in which the strongest combination would be most likely to prevail, whether it consisted of those who support-ed or of those who resisted the general authority.[2]

_____

2 Alexander Hamilton, James Madison, and John Jay, The Federalist Papers, No.16, (Mineola, NY: Dover Publications, 2014), p.73)

50

This notion was contrary to George Washington's belief that the United States should not have a standing army. Alexander Hamilton also argued that there must be a national court system:

> The majesty of the national authority must be manifested through the medium of the courts of justice…It must, in short, possess all the means, and have a right to resort to all the methods, of executing the power with which it is intrusted, that are possessed and exercised by the governments of the particular States.[3]

Without a doubt, Hamilton's view of government reflects the United States' political system's current structure. His arguments held considerable weight at the Constitutional Convention in 1787.

On the other hand, the Anti-Federalists held the view that there was no point in going to war with England if we were only going to adopt an identical form of national government here. Alexander Hamilton did not hold back in voicing his fear of giving states (and individuals) too much power. His arguments rarely answer the question: what if the national government abuses its power? In his mind, unrestricted ambition for power comes from the passions of individuals and the state, with no ability whatsoever to police itself:

> The regulation of the mere domestic police of a State appears to me to hold out slender allurements to ambition. Commerce, finance, negotiation, and war seem to comprehend all the objects which have charms for minds governed by that passion; and all the powers necessary to those objects ought in the first instance to be lodged in the national depository.[4]

Simply stated, Hamilton contends that the State's ambitions will interfere with the regulation of what he has deemed national priorities. At the same time, he believes the smaller states can only enforce local policing of things like private justice between citizens, supervision of agriculture, and "other similar things of that nature." He continues to state that it would not be in the national government's best interest to regulate these affairs:

> It is therefore improbable that there should exist a disposi-

[3] Ibid. P. 75

[4] Ibid. P. 77

51

tion in the federal councils to usurp the powers with which they are connected; because the attempt to exercise those powers would be as troublesome as it would be nugatory... [it] would contribute nothing to the dignity, to the importance, or to the splendor of the national government.[5]

Hamilton fails to see the risk that an all-powerful federal government poses to its citizens. However, the issue is expanded upon in other papers, specifically those written by James Madison, and are eventually finalized in the first articles of the Constitution as it currently stands today.

In Federalist Paper Number 41, James Madison outlines his "General view of the powers conferred by the Constitution." At this point in the dialogue, the threat of expansive power from the national government is examined. Madison states:

...in every political institution, a power to advance the public happiness involves a discretion which may be misapplied and abused...in all cases where power is to be conferred, the point first to be decided is whether such a power be necessary to the public good; as the next will be in case of an affirmative decision, to guard as effectually as possible against a perversion of the power to the public detriment.[6]

Madison was wary of political power no matter which area of government, national or local, judicial, or legislative. Nevertheless, at the onset of this paper, Madison views the Constitution from the same vantage point that Hamilton does, and that is a document whereby specific restraints are imposed upon the states, and all national powers are distributed equally among the branches of government. Madison proclaims:

The Constitution proposed by the convention may be considered under two general points of view. The FIRST relates to the sum or quantity of power which it vests in the government, including the restraints imposed on the States. The SECOND, to the particular structure of the government and the distribution of this power among its several branches.[7]

Anti-Federalists allege that Hamilton and his allies have failed to address the ambition for power at the national level and

[5] Ibid. P. 78

[6] Alexander Hamilton, James Madison, and John Jay, The Federalist Papers, No. 41, (Mineola, NY: Dover Publications, 2014), p.195)

[7] Ibid.

its tendency to intervene in state affairs. Luckily, we have the historical advantage of hindsight. Which sentiments will prove accurate? More importantly, which sentiments are in alignment with the original ideas that inspired the Declaration of Independence and the revolution that followed?

In "Brutus No. 7" written February 7th, 1788, it is alleged that the ratified Constitution's structure is inherently flawed from the beginning, immediately stripping power from the states:

> The first object declared to be in view is "To form a perfect union." It is to be observed, it is not an union of states or bodies corporate; had this been the case the existence of the state governments, might have been secured. But it is a union of this kind perfect, it is necessary to abolish all inferior governments, and to give the general one compleat legislative, executive, and judicial powers to every purpose. The courts therefore will establish it as a rule in explaining the Constitution to give it such a construction as will best tend to perfect the union or take from the state governments every power of either making or executing laws...I might proceed to the other clause, in the preamble, and it would appear by a consideration of all of them separately, as it does by taking them together, that if the spirit of this system is to be known from its declared end and design in the preamble, its spirit is to subvert and abolish all the powers of the state government and to embrace every object to which any government extends.[8]

He continues:

> Any person who will peruse the 8th section with attention, in which most of the powers are enumerated, will perceive that they either expressly or by implication extend to almost every thing about which any legislative power can be employed.[9]

From Brutus' perspective, the Constitution gives too much power to the federal body of government as a whole as compared to its subservient state governments. He sees no end to its powers. He has correctly observed that the line "to form a more perfect union" is referencing the Union of "We the People of the United

[8] Ralph Ketcham, The Anti-Federalist Papers ; and the Constitutional Convention Debates (New York, NY: Signet Classic, 2003), "Brutus, XII," p. 318)

[9] Ibid. p. 319.

States," not a union of individual States, but the people of the United States as a whole. Is he correct that the Constitution gives too much power to the Federal body of government? To confirm these assertions, it is vital to examine the Constitution further, specifically the 8th section.

The line "promote the general Welfare" in the preamble has been interpreted in multiple ways to suit the Federal government's interests. A modern interpretation would lead one to believe this means food stamps and government housing. Unfortunately, some of the liberal courts have interpreted it in this way too. The wording of the clause has allowed for plenty of room for debate. The crucial decisions made concerning the lines within Section 8 of the Constitution have relied on the interpretations of the preamble. Many do not realize that every word within the Constitution is considered when making a Supreme Court decision. Alexander Hamilton believed this clause gave the national government the power to spend indefinitely to maintain the general welfare. At the same time, James Madison contended these powers were limited only to the Constitution's enumerated powers, and the clause cannot be interpreted in the broadest sense.

The first clause of Article I, Section 8, also known as the "General Welfare Clause," states, "The Congress shall have Power to lay and collect Taxes, Duties, Imposts, and Excises, to pay the Debts and provide for the common Defence and general Welfare of the United States." In *United States v. Butler (1936)*, the U.S. Supreme Court terminated a federal agricultural program because a specific congressional power over agricultural production appeared nowhere in the Constitution. The local courts in Butler argued that the spending program violated a reserved power to the states under the 10th amendment.[10] The court summarized:

A tax, in the general understanding and in the strict constitutional sense, is an exaction for the support of Government; the term does not connote the expropriation of money from one group to be expended for another, as a necessary means in a plan of regulation, such as the plan for regulating agricultural production set up in the Agricultural Adjustment

[10] "General Welfare," Federal, Court, Congress, and Spending - JRank Articles, accessed August 18, 2020, https://law.jrank.org/pages/7116/General-Welfare.html)

Act...The Agricultural Adjustment Act does not purport to regulate transactions in interstate or foreign commerce; and the Government in this case does not attempt to sustain it under the commerce clause of the Constitution.[11]

And, most importantly:

The power to tax and spend is a separate and distinct power; its exercise is not confined to the fields committed to Congress by the other enumerated grants of power; but it is limited by the requirement that it shall be exercised to provide for the *general welfare* of the United States.[12]

The Supreme Court held Madison's opinion in so far as the federal government cannot exceed its enumerated powers to tax and regulate foreign and interstate commerce. However, the ruling did uphold Hamilton's view that the power to tax, spend, and regulate is a separate and unique power by itself, allowing Congress to determine specific needs based on the General Welfare clause. The argument that the local officials in Butler made was essentially the wrong argument. The court ruled that the feds do have the power to enter into the arena of regulating local agriculture; they just found the program's structure to be unconstitutional, specifically the forced transfer of funds within the agricultural market. The ruling set a legal precedent for expansive regulatory power at the federal level, regardless of whether it impacted each state's policies.

It is undeniable that the interpretation of the General Welfare clause has been expanded on over time. Brutus finalizes his thoughts about the clause:

This will certainly give the first clause in that article a construction which I confess I think the most natural and grammatical one, to authorise the Congress to do any thing which in their judgement will tend to provide for the general welfare, and this amounts to the same thing as general and unlimited powers of legislation in all cases.[13]

His views are utterly antithetical to the Constitution and the beliefs of the Founders. They believed they had created the

---

[11] Syllabus to United States v. Butler, 401 US 1 (1935).

[12] Ibid.

[13] Ralph Ketcham, The Anti-Federalist Papers ; and the Constitutional Convention Debates (New York, NY: Signet Classic, 2003), "Brutus, XII," p. 319)

perfect-imperfect document, with a separation of powers. Brutus contends that intrinsic flaws within the document will disband all three branches into a unified oligarchy, inevitably creating the same type of government that we fought for independence from in 1776.

The other clause within the Constitution that is notorious for expanding federal power is the "Commerce Clause," which reads, "[The Congress shall have Power] To regulate Commerce with foreign Nations, and among the several States, and with the Indian Tribes." After reading the text of this enumerated power, imagine all of the areas of daily life that fall under the scope of the term "commerce." Without a doubt, the People of the United States in 1787 handed over a blank check to their future Congressional leaders.

Over time, the Supreme Court has expanded this definition due to the fact crafty politicians found creative arguments for anything that could positively or negatively affect commerce among the states so that eventually they could control both intrastate and interstate commerce. The takeover began with the Interstate Commerce Act of 1887, which created the Interstate Commerce Commission.

In *Gibbons v. Ogden (1824),* the Supreme Court ruled that New York could not ban a steamship company from operating in its waters, affirming the enumerated power to regulate commerce between the states. Transportation is arguably the most logical situation the founders were considering when writing these edicts. In a far cry from this case, the commerce clause was used in 2017 to order prostitution restitution in an international sex trafficking operation with *Damion St. Patrick Baston v. United States,* where the court ruled that a prostitute was owed restitution for the money she gave to her Jamaican pimp due to the fact it "substantially affects commerce between the U.S. and other countries."[14] In the singlehanded dissent, Justice Clarence Thomas noted that with that type of logic, Congress could regulate virtually any activity worldwide, including "working conditions in factories in China, pollution from power plants in

---

[14] John-Michael Seibler, "Commerce Clause Just Keeps On Expanding," The Heritage Foundation, accessed August 18, 2020, https://www.heritage.org/government-regulation/commentary/commerce-clause-just-keeps-expanding)

India, or agricultural methods on farms in France."[15]

In *Upstate Citizens v. United States*, the Supreme Court ruled that the Commerce Clause allowed the Secretary of the Interior to transfer 13,000 acres of land to the Oneida Indian Nation, the plaintiffs, who argued the clause did not permit the transfer, lost. Once again, the lone ranger Justice Thomas dissented when he observed that the Founders understood this clause "to give Congress the limited authority to 'regulate trade with Indian tribes living beyond state borders,'" not "the power to take any state land and strip the State of almost all sovereign power over it."[16]

In PETPO v. U.S. Fish & Wildlife Service, over 200 Utahans argued that Congress' authority to regulate commerce among the several states does not justify federal protections for the Utah prairie dog. The federal regulation that would ban harming these rodents and their habitat was shot down by the District Court, where the appellate court later ruled for the government. The Supreme Court declined to hear the case in a victory for the landowners.[17]

These cases provide clear insight into the government's constant attempts to expand its regulatory power under the guise of the poorly worded General Welfare Clause and Commerce Clause. The word "commerce" encompasses multiple functions for local, state, and national governments. Throughout our daily lives, we are continually engaged in some sort of commerce.

This atmosphere for continued growth in the government's size has allowed for infringements in other areas as well. In a 2018 poll of 1000 Americans, over 82 percent were in favor of term limits on members of Congress.[18] In the case *U.S. Term Limits, Inc. v. Thornton (1995)*, the Supreme Court ruled that states cannot impose qualifications for prospective members of the U.S. Congress. According to Justice John Paul Stevens, Arkansas' Amendment 73 was ruled unconstitutional because it:

15 Ibid.

16 Ibid.

17 Ibid.

18 "M&A Poll: Voters Overwhelmingly Support Term Limits for Congress," McLaughlin & Associates, accessed August 18, 2020, https://mclaughlinonline.com/2018/02/08/ma-poll-voters-overwhelmingly-support-term-limits-for-congress/)

violate[s] an [third] idea central to this basic principle: that the right to choose representatives belongs not to the States, but to the People…The Congress of the United States, therefore, is not a confederation of nations in which separate sovereigns are represented by appointed delegates, but is instead a body composed of representatives of the people.

Unfortunately for the *people who live in the States*, Justice Stevens is correct in his analysis of the U.S. Constitution. Due to the fact the document delegates specific powers, including election rules for members of the House of Representatives and the Senate, states cannot implement their own rules. Does the Supreme Court's ruling against term limits for Congress mean that the ruling itself is just? It is at this point in the discussion that we must return to the Anti-Federalist Papers.

Brutus was prophetic when he proclaimed [the Constitution's] "spirit is to subvert and abolish all the powers of the state government and to embrace every object to which any government extends." His conclusion that the federal government would regularly expand its power is correct. In essence, he challenges the concept that the Union, or "the People," have more interest in control of the government than the States. He correctly observes that this is a concept that puts the federal government as the supreme enforcer of the supreme law of the land. The debate is whether states' rights would stand the test of time. The *PETPO* case is only one of many other examples of overreach by the Federal government, most of it concerning land and property rights. What is the point of the 10th amendment if the federal government's definition of its enumerated powers continually expands? This is the sole question at the heart of the Anti-Federalist arguments.

The current size of the Federal Government has extended far past its constitutional bounds. Without looking at every Congressional program, we can see the growth in the size of local, state, and federal government in the government data and the studies from other scholars who have looked at budget reports with private contractors. Of course, the government data cannot solely be relied upon.

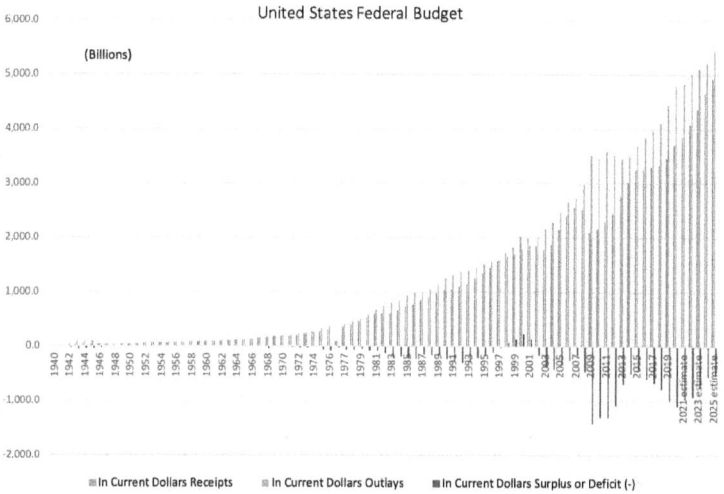

Figure (A) U.S. Federal Budget, Accessed August, 2020.

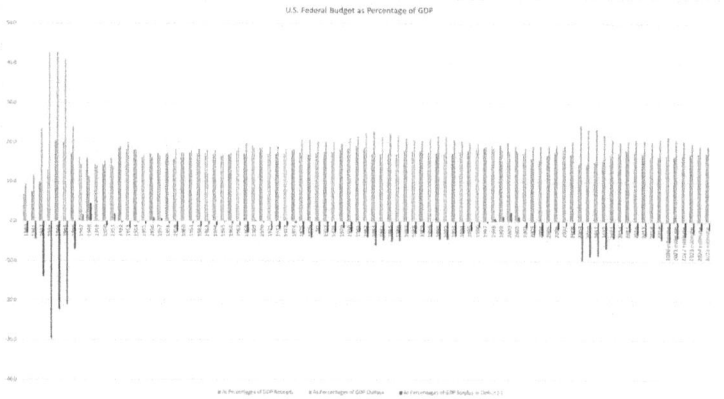

Figure (B) U.S. Federal Budget as Percentage of GDP, Accessed August, 2020.

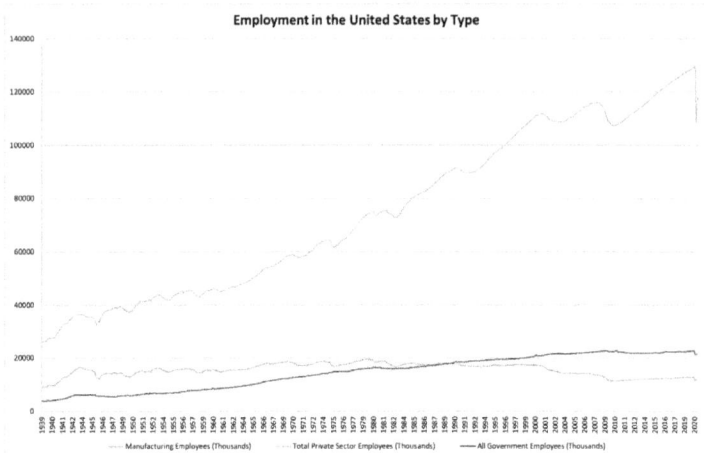

Figure (C) Employment in the United States by Type, Bureau of Labor Statistics, Accessed August, 2020.

In a remarkable observation, there are more government employees in the United States than manufacturing employees. The data shows that the United States economy stopped manufacturing goods over thirty years ago and has not looked back. At the same time, government debt levels continue to reach historic highs.

This data highlights the U.S.'s marked transition from a Constitutional free-market based Republic to a massive bureaucratic socialist dictatorship. The Democratic party today is not the Democratic party of yesterday. Both parties allege against each other, "this isn't your parent's [insert party here.]" Both of them are right. Today, the Democratic Party platform resembles the Communist platform of the 1950s. This sentiment is especially true if you already view America as a socialist state, where the national economy is controlled by a Federal Reserve that is always distorting the economy, and with social welfare expenditures that consistently increase every year:

- In 1900 the government spent $10 billion on social welfare.
- In 1950 the government spent $130 billion on social welfare.
- In 1988 the government spent $980 billion on

social welfare.[19]

- In 2011, the government spent $1.03 trillion on social welfare.[20]

In 1990, studies showed that it would have cost $75 billion to bring every family with income below the poverty level above that benchmark. The government was spending two-and-a-half times what would be needed to "end" poverty in America. It is undeniable that these policy programs are failing as the government increases in size.

Although the Foundation for Economic Education's article highlighted the necessary data to criticize progressive social policies, it lamented the fact that these expenditures were taken from the federal defense budget. Herein lies the big lie from "conservative" politicians: both parties spend into oblivion to serve their corrupt interests, one party serves the interests of financiers for welfare and dependency, the other serves the interests of the corrupt military-industrial complex.

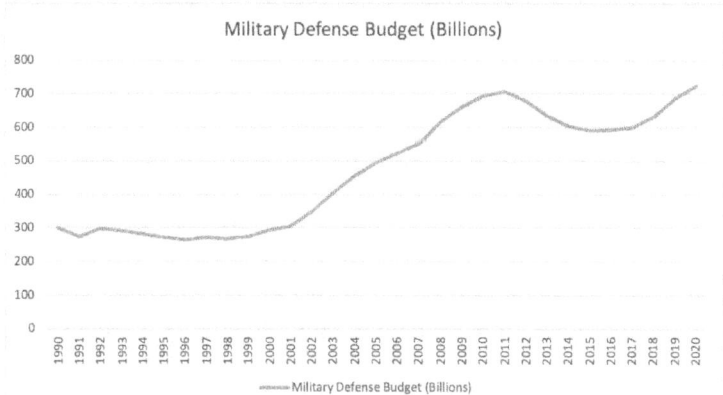

Figure (D) Military Defense Budget, U.S. Budget, Accessed August, 2020.

Both parties have one common foundation within their ideologies: the core tenets of the Precautionary Principle. When one looks further, it is clear that the theory is not relegated to environmental regulation and protection. Both conservative and

[19] Stephen Moore, "The Growth of Government in America: Stephen Moore," FEE Freeman Article, April 01, 1993, accessed August 18, 2020, https://fee.org/articles/the-growth-of-government-in-america/)

[20] S. Rep. "CRS Report: Welfare Spending the Largest Item in the Federal Budget," 112th (2011).

democratic parties alike cannot resist the knee-jerk reaction to prevent crises, whether in the economic, ecological, or geopolitical arena. It is literally at the point where they are trying to play God in all areas of life.

We have seen the failures of this ideology both domestically and on the world stage. At home, democrat regulation to raise cigarette taxes to "prevent youth smoking and smoking abroad" led to the death of Eric Garner, a man selling individual cigarettes in New York City at a lower rate after purchasing them in bulk from a state with lower taxes. The case was a perfect example of unintended consequences from over-zealous bureaucrats who think they have the power to affect our individual decisions. The devout Marxist Denver City Council raised the tobacco age to 21 and raised taxes on tobacco products in 2019.[21] In 2020 after the George Floyd national uproar, Colorado Governor Jared Polis signed a police accountability bill.[22] It is said that excessive regulation leads to excessive force, and the backward logic from Democrat politicians in this example proves that point.

The neoconservative wing of the Republican Party has controlled the party's direction and its national platform for the last 40 years. Any time that a true conservative denounces the United States' reckless foreign policy, they are immediately labeled as an isolationist. The best example of this is the twice failed campaigns of former Congressman Ron Paul from Texas:

> The 1%, those who live off us, those who live in the military-industrial complex, and they are living off the government, and they control the government, the Federal Reserve, and the banking system, THAT 1% needs to be called upon and we need to get rid of that by getting rid of the power of big government.[23]

Since 9/11, we have seen our national debt explode by 11 trillion for two unconstitutional wars. What was once America's "Lon-

---

[21] "NEWS: Denver Becomes 11th City in Colorado to Raise Tobacco Age to 21," Tobacco Free Colorado, October 04, 2019, |PAGE|, accessed August 18, 2020, https://www.tobaccofreeco.org/product/vaping-and-ecigs/denver-becomes-11th-city-in-colorado-to-raise-tobacco-age-to-21/)

[22] "Colorado Governor Signs Sweeping Police Accountability Bill into Law. Here's How It Will Change Law Enforcement.," The Colorado Sun, accessed August 18, 2020, https://coloradosun.com/2020/06/19/colorado-police-accountability-bill-becomes-law/)

[23] Speech by Ron Paul, Secession and Liberty, Mises Institute, February 2, 2015, accessed September 2, 2020, https://www.youtube.com/watch?v=g36Ef5Fvkok, 31:00)

gest War," in Vietnam, is a far-gone memory. We have been in Afghanistan now for 19 years. In short, neoconservatives argue that America must be an active nation, or else the world will fall apart. Since then, the world has yet to feel like it did before this cataclysmic event.

Our perverted interpretation of the Constitution over time and the inherent flaws of the document itself have ultimately given birth to multiple generations of control freaks. The Supreme Court and Americans alike have confused the terms "General Welfare" with "Social Welfare." The Commerce Clause has been used to extend the government's hand into every single activity of our daily lives. In doing so, other Constitutional provisions that appear to be hardened, such as "Congress must declare war," have been eviscerated.

The bureaucratic state has yet to reach its peak. In the ultimate regulatory singularity, both the neoconservative and Marxist elements within the United States are merging to form one oligarchy. We are witnessing all regulatory bodies converge to create one unilateral system for not just the United States but the entire world. Now, we can comprehend its early beginnings.

IV

The Perfect Disaster: The Hegelian Dialectic and the Economic Collapse of 2008

"You never let a serious crisis go to waste. And what I mean by that is [it's] an opportunity to do things that you think you could not do before."
Rahm Emanuel, former advisor to President Barack Obama

We have seen government bureaucrats' mentality when it comes to offering solutions and how they come to find them. If there is a problem, there must be a law or policy to correct it. If there is not a law or bureaucracy to enforce it, create it. Of course, to have a proposed solution, there must be a perceived problem, correct? To fully comprehend the precautionary principle and its effectiveness in assessing societal calamities, one must examine the philosophical history of what scholars call "The Hegelian Dialectic." The dialectic is based on Hegel's logic model, and the concept of the Precautionary Principle can be viewed from this perspective. If we finish the logical statement, if there is not a present problem but a perceived need for a specific government bureaucracy, the natural order would be to create one, yes? Therein lies the final position of the precautionary principle and its partner, the Hegelian Dialectic.

In 2008, America experienced the worse economic collapse since the Great Depression. As expected, the government bureaucrats went to work crafting legislation to mitigate the economic crisis, and a new social and economic order rose out of the ashes. The definition of the "American Dream" was altered forever, inexorably paving the way for a new reality for America's baby boomers and millennials alike. The question must be asked: did the economic recession of 2008 serve as a catalyst for a new social and economic order? With further analysis, it will become evident the change in economic demographics worldwide allowed for a new economic structure to develop, redefining the banking structure, and providing a "new" interpretation of individual property rights.

The economic recession in 2008 came as a shocking surprise for most Americans. The main financial sector affected was the housing market. The crash began in the housing markets with the collapse of major financial players like the Lehman Brothers and permeated throughout the rest of the market. Millions of Americans lost their homes. From 2008 to 2010, just under 9 million foreclosure filings were issued.[12] Nevada led the country with a home foreclosure rate of just over 10% at the height of the crisis.[3] According to the United States Bureau of Labor Statistics, Between January 2008 and February 2010, employment fell by 8.8 million—the largest absolute decline in the series' history...Manufacturing employment fell 2.0 million, or 14.6 percent, from December 2007 through June 2009.[4] This economic historical record dates back to 1939. The DOW Jones had lost almost fifty percent of its values from September 2007 to June 2009.[5] As the carnage was unfolding, the US government intervened with unprecedented action with massive bailouts for US auto companies and other major financial institutions. Most Americans thought that the bailout ended with $700 Billion given to the big banks (JP Morgan, Goldman Sachs, and others). Forbes reported in 2015 that the US government is actually on the hook for $16.8 trillion, with $4.7 trillion being paid out thus far.[6] Without a doubt, the recession would have direct and underlying consequences for many more years to come.

Many Americans lost all of their retirement savings after the 2008 economic crisis, and food stamp usage hit all-time highs during those years. Economic inequality rose starkly has

[1] Les Christie, "Foreclosures up a Record 81% in 2008," CNNMoney (Cable News Network, January 15, 2009), https://money.cnn.com/2009/01/15/real_estate/millions_in_foreclosure/)

[2] Bianna Golodryga, ABC News (ABC News Network, January 12, 2011), https://abcnews.go.com/Business/2010-record-29-million-foreclosures/story?id=12602271)

[3] Steve Kerch, "2009 Foreclosures Hit Record High," MarketWatch (MarketWatch, January 14, 2010), https://www.marketwatch.com/story/foreclosures-top-record-in-2009-no-end-in-sight-2010-01-14)

[4] Christopher J Goodman and Steven M Mance, "Employment Loss and the 2007–09 Recession: an Overview" (Bureau of Labor Statistics, April 2011), https://www.bls.gov/opub/mlr/2011/04/art1full.pdf, p.6)

[5] "Finance," DOW Jones Industrial Average Chart (Google), accessed March 17, 2020, https://www.google.com/finance)

[6] Mike Collins, "The Big Bank Bailout," Forbes (Forbes Magazine, July 14, 2015), https://www.forbes.com/sites/mikecollins/2015/07/14/the-big-bank-bailout/#7b5403e92d83)

remained constant since the crisis, and homelessness rates in major cities across the US continue to rise or remain steady. These metrics represent the true standard of living in the United States. Furthermore, they directly reflect the average American's efficacy to reach what most people define as "the American dream" or the prospect of retirement. People did not only lose their jobs during these years. The National Poverty Center reported that between the peak of the stock market from October 9, 2007, and March 2009, equity prices fell 50 percent. Retirement participants in IRA accounts and 401(k) plans saw a decrease in value of over $2.8 trillion. Their report also concluded that before the financial crisis, Americans have faced a consistent trend of working longer for less, which has remained consistent since the early 1980s.[7] In short, Americans are working longer, earning less, and saving less.

The economic crisis has forced many to become more dependent on the helping hand of the government. From 2008 to 2009, the United States saw a 35 percent increase in food stamp use.[8] These costs directly reflect the increased amount of participants in the program and the rise of economic inequality. According to the US Census Bureau, the gap between the richest and the poorest US households is now the largest it has been in the past 50 years. Due to the fact the economic crisis began due to systemic problems in the housing and financial markets, it is no surprise that the United States has seen a sizeable increase in homelessness rates throughout its major cities. The majority of these populations exist in cities like Los Angeles and New York City. Both cities have seen rent increases of twenty to thirty-five percent.[9] California alone has seen a 16.4% increase in homelessness, which led to a 3% increase on a national level from 2018 to

[7] Alicia H Munnell and Matthew S Rutledge, "The Effects of the Great Recession on the Retirement Security of Older Workers"(National Poverty Center, March 1, 2013), http://npc.umich.edu/publications/u/2013-03-npc-working-paper.pdf, p.3-5)

[8] "SNAP Data Tables," USDA, accessed March 17, 2020, https://www.fns.usda.gov/pd/supplemental-nutrition-assistance-program-snap)

[9] Owen Daugherty, "Homelessness Rates Increase in US for Second Straight Year," TheHill (The Hill, December 17, 2018), https://thehill.com/blogs/blog-briefing-room/news/421684-homelessness-rates-increase-in-us-for-second-straight-year)

2019.[10] One only has to look at the number of tents in their cities to see the national homelessness crisis's real state. To properly understand the true causes of the 2008 economic downturn, we must identify key events before the start of the recession that caused instability throughout the market. When one looks closer, it will become apparent that the entire US economy is a house of cards built upon fraudulent schemes invented by greedy bankers and protected by corrupt politicians and financial regulators.

The US financial system has become overly complicated, especially for the average consumer. This is not by accident—it is designed to confuse the American populace so that they do not see the other hand stealing out of their back pockets. The regulatory environment has promoted a symbiotic relationship between regulator and banker. Those that work in the SEC often worked in the financial sector, and vice versa. The 2008 economic crash was the direct result of this toxic relationship. The existence of this relationship is the direct result of a failed ideology in Keynesian economic theory and the greed that promulgated from its execution in national and global markets. The problem has remained consistent in the American financial system since the early 90s, where housing markets became a tool for artificial economic stimulation. The 2008 recession was the direct result of artificial stimulation in the housing markets and the fraudulent bets placed on the market through the use of derivatives or mortgage-backed securities.

The problems began when Bill Clinton and George W. Bush artificially stimulated the housing markets by lessening the requirements to obtain a home loan, while also allowing consumers to turn their homes into "mini-banks" with excessive home equity lines of credit with artificially controlled interest rates from the Federal Reserve. The 1992 housing bill mandated that Fannie Mae and Freddie Mac make 30% of their mortgage purchases be affordable-housing loans. Among other regulations passed during the Clinton era, this bill pushed financial institutions into making subprime loans. When George W. Bush approved the "American Downpayment Initiative" in 2003,

[10] Lola Fadulu, "Homelessness Rises 2.7 Percent, Driven by California's Crisis, Report Says," The New York Times (The New York Times, December 20, 2019), https://www.nytimes.com/2019/12/20/us/politics/homelessness-trump-california.html)

low-income Americans suddenly had access to loan funds they previously did not have access to. Consumers had access to down payment assistance that would cover bank processing fees, title fees, and even the down payment itself, with no regard for consumer credit history. The big banks had no problem under-writing these loans—after all, they had the US government's backing. According to the Federal Reserve, from 1979 to 2006, the mortgage delinquency rate averaged 1.7 percent. By the second quarter of 2008, this rate had surged to 4.5 percent.[11] The entire system became a house of cards as those who truly could not afford to purchase a home suddenly became new homeowners.

Now, imagine this house of cards with a dining room table and another house of cards sitting upon it. Enter the financial derivatives market. Derivatives are financial products that are *derived* from other financial products. In the case of the housing market, mortgage-backed securities are a financial product sold among other investors comprised of multiple home mortgage loans. These mortgage-backed securities are *consolidated* once again into Collateralized Debt Obligations (CDOs). These products are simply a collection of home loans, sold at a higher price on an individual basis. They are both sold individually and collectively on an open market. When the FED artificially induces the market with low-interest rates, down payment assistance, and low-credit requirements, all they have done is build a financial product based on the decisions of a bunch of low-income consumers who may or may not be able to pay their monthly mortgage bill. In 2008, subprime mortgages for low-income consumers brought down the entire national market and eventually, the global market. Banks took advantage of the poor. Governments looked the other way and often promoted the fraudulent activity. Instead of offering comparable homes for low-income individuals, they induced these folks into buying homes they could not afford.

For the American consumer, the 2008 recession stole their income, retirement, and possibly their future. For the globalist banker, the 2008 recession boosted the banks' profits, CEO bonuses, and their overall position in the market. As those

[11] Chris Mayer, Karen Pence, and Shane M. Sherlund, "The Rise in Mortgage Defaults" (Federal Reserve, November 1, 2008), https://www.federalreserve.gov/pubs/feds/2008/200859/200859pap.pdf, p.2)

at the US Treasury stated in 2008, the big banks were "too big to fail." They knew they would come out on top in the end. The CEOs were given big bonuses for the financial institutions that did fail, even as their doors shut. The CDO product still exists, banks have once again relaxed their requirements for obtaining a home loan, and the market has expanded to levels unseen before. However, there was a massive consolidation of economic power in the process. America has become a country of haves and have-nots. The American financial market can no longer be described as "free" if we are bailing out those who caused the financial disaster in the first place. We have essentially rewarded bad behavior. We have created undeserving monopolies out of thin air.

For these reasons, it is obvious something *new* has come out of the 2008 economic recession. A *new* definition of what constitutes a "free" market. A *new* definition of what constitutes fraud and manipulation. Unfortunately, the average American believes what occurred in 2008 was due to unfettered capitalism. In reality, it was the exact opposite. The 2008 recession was sanctioned and possibly induced by the US government. If we have a poor understanding of what occurred in 2008, we undoubtedly will have a poor understanding of what constitutes a solution. When we mislabel what occurred   blatant fraud perpetrated by the US government and big banks against the American people—with lazy, ignorant descriptions of what occurred, we end up with a perverted perspective; a perspective that is blind to the economic and political situation that is unfolding before us. The US government has one job: to serve as a referee in the open market to prevent cheating and fraud, not to help foster an environment that does the exact opposite. With that being said, what is the new economic and political environment that will replace the one that existed before 2008?

President Obama's former advisor Rahm Emanuel said that "we must never let any crisis go to waste."[12] He then elaborated that there are certain things you can do politically that you would not have been able to do otherwise had it not been for a certain crisis. The national poverty center pointed out in their study that the quality of life for the American worker has been on the decline for the last 40 years. However, there has not been

[12] Jack Rosenthal, "A Terrible Thing to Waste," The New York Times (The New York Times, July 31, 2009), https://www.nytimes.com/2009/08/02/magazine/02FOB-onlanguage-t.html)

a shock to the American financial system like the 2008 recession since the Great Depression. The series of events during the financial crisis—specifically the crash in equity markets and the collapse of financial institutions worldwide—created a power vacuum for governments to fill. Indeed, American regulators and financiers alike would take advantage of the crisis at hand.

Rahm is tapping into an ancient philosophical theory developed from the ideas of Georg Wilhelm Friedrich Hegel (1770-1831), a German philosopher who studied at the height of the Enlightenment period. Hegel was known for inspiring other German philosophers like Karl Marx and Friedrich Nietzsche. It is here where the ideology and the strategy to utilize the ideology in practice come together. Philosophy will always be the primary source of inspiration for all political theories and their subsequent implementation. Hegel's philosophical works inspired several logical theorems; however, philosopher Johann Gottlieb Fichte developed the concept that Rahm and many other leaders have latched on to. The logical "thesis-antithesis-synthesis" theorem has proven to be the most effective in both American politics and European politics. Because Fichte's conclusions were solely based on Hegel's theories, Hegel has popularly been credited with this logical equation.

The "thesis-antithesis-synthesis" theory can be simplified to "problem-reaction-solution." Fichte based his model after Hegel's "Being-Nothing-Becoming," as written in his work the *Science of Logic*. Julie E. Maybee of Stanford University translates it best: "To Become is to go from Being to Nothing or from Nothing to Being, or is, as Hegel puts it, 'the immediate vanishing of the one in the other.'"[13] Maybee also translates Fichte's model: "…Being is the positive moment or thesis, Nothing is the negative moment or antithesis, and Becoming is the moment of *aufheben* or synthesis—the concept that cancels and preserves, or unifies and combines, Being and Nothing."[14] With all equations translated, it looks like this:

Being → Nothing → Becoming
Thesis → Antithesis → Synthesis
Problem → Reaction → Solution

[13] Julie E. Maybee, "Hegel's Dialectics," Stanford Encyclopedia of Philosophy (Stanford University, June 3, 2016), https://plato.stanford.edu/entries/hegel-dialectics/)

[14] Ibid.

What philosophers like Marx and politicians who subscribed to them had realized was that they could interpret and act on these events in no specific order. This revelation is precisely what Rahm Emanuel meant when he said the government could do much more in the event of an unnamed crisis. He did not outright say it—but it can be directly implied that if no crisis exists, one can be created to serve as a catalyst for enacting some agenda or piece of legislation.

In the case of the 2008 economic crisis, the theorem can easily be applied, when it is understood that the final piece of the equation has yet to be implemented:

Thesis → Antithesis → Synthesis
Problem → Reaction → Solution
2008 Economic Crisis (Problem) → Bailouts/ill-fated re-forms/lack of reforms (Reaction) → Solution (?)

When viewing this equation while listening to Rahm Emanuel's words, the logic reveals itself. Many historians and political scientists have argued that this has been the mode of thought for the global elite for many years. Hegel's dialectics have inspired the analysis behind the notion of "false flag theory," the observation that many nations throughout history have attacked their fleets to provide a contextual pretext for war. If this type of logic has been observed on the battlefield, there is no denying that leaders of nations would use economics to manipulate the chessboard.

In the case of the 2008 recession, the proof for future damage to the US economic and political structure is in the antithesis piece of the equation or the reaction. Since the 2008 recession, the Federal Reserve's assets went from $870 Billion in August 2007 to $4.5 trillion in early 2015. As of January 2020, the FED's balance sheet stands at $4.1 trillion.[15] In essence, the FED is buying up junk bonds, mortgage-backed securities, treasury securities, repurchase agreements, and other forms of debt

[15] "Total Assets of the Federal Reserve," Board of Governors of the Federal Reserve System (Federal Reserve), accessed March 17, 2020, https://www.federalreserve.gov/monetarypolicy/bst_recenttrends.htm)

from major financial institutions to support the market. Think of it this way—banks profit off of the sale of this debt, so the FED is essentially printing money for them. The problem lies with the fact that this economy is based entirely on low-interest rates. We have seen several attempts to raise interest rates; however, the economy immediately responded poorly. Politics have overtaken commonsense mathematical logic when it comes to US budgetary policy.

Has the US curtailed spending in light of the financial crisis? Of course not! As of January 2020, the United States' current debt totals at just over $23 trillion.[16] Every President and Congress since the 2008 crisis has built up trillion-dollar deficits year-over-year.[17] President Bush increased upon his predecessor Bill Clinton's budget numbers, and Obama surpassed Bush's. President Trump is also racking up a large amount of debt, which will not lead to a balanced budget in any of our lifetimes. However, he has decreased deficits when compared to his predecessors. The spending cuts are not enough, and if interest rates ever rise, the US economy is in serious trouble. The Wall Street Journal has reported that the US national debt will rise to 98% of GDP by 2030.

With these facts in mind, it is necessary to ponder whether a new economic and political order lays on the horizon. The proposed solutions to the 2008 economic crisis have been outright failures. The data shows that a new economic realignment has occurred, and it has not been for the better. Some reforms have occurred under the Trump administration; however, much of it paints a too-little-too-late picture. Trump is still heavily reliant on the FED's printing press, in light of his tax cuts and removal of red tape for businesses. Peter Schiff, an economist and hedge fund investor that was one of the few to predict the recession is not content with the US response to the recession:

> We haven't had actual economic growth…it is like the field of dreams, they assume that because this idea is in their minds, that it is reality. As long as we can keep the interest rates low, the payments on the national debt can remain

[16] "US National Debt Clock : Real Time," US National Debt Clock : Real Time, accessed March 17, 2020, https://www.usdebtclock.org/)

[17] Bob Bryan, "The US National Debt Just Pushed Past $22 Trillion - Here's How Trump's $2 Trillion in Debt Compares with Obama, Bush, and Clinton," Business Insider (Business Insider, February 20, 2019), https://www.businessinsider.com/trump-national-debt-deficit-compared-to-obama-bush-clinton-2019-2)

tiny…but we are beginning to see inflation. People are thinking this is the strength in the economy when in reality, it is the weakness in the dollar… The tax cuts will be overwhelmed by the increase in the cost of living… Interest rates will forcibly rise when the FED runs out of options.[18]

The 2008 recession has and will serve as the ultimate catalyst for an economic and political realignment that the United States has never seen before.

When the Hegelian Dialectic is placed on the table with the Precautionary Principle, the theories directly mirror each other. The precautionary principle promotes the idea that we must enact precautionary measures to prevent crises that have not occurred yet. In other words, it recognizes well-researched political and societal regulation as a feasible achievement and necessary response to prevent absolute catastrophe. When viewed through Hegel and Fichte's thesis-antithesis-synthesis deduction, the precautionary principle fits in the role of "thesis" and "synthesis." It represents the "thesis" in so far as it poses a potential problem, and it also represents the "synthesis" in that it also represents the final solution in the equation to this potential problem. The "antithesis" would indicate the possible consequences or inadequate/negative response to the problem.

The 2008 recession represents the problem, and we have failed as a nation to develop an appropriate response to it. Politicians and financial regulators will rely on the precautionary principle's tenets to create new regulations and incentives in their attempts to prop up the American economy. When these options fail, American citizens and politicians alike will clamor for more government intervention. What will this intervention look like? What will the scale of this intervention be? If history has shown us anything, it will likely involve more bailouts, more consolidation of power, and more monopolization. The American people will likely have an overbearing and powerful federal government enforce a new socio-economic and political regulatory structure that will test the American political system to its limits in the coming years. Luckily for us, those in power have told us exactly how the new political structure will be enforced. It represents the

---

[18] *Peter Schiff: The Next Financial Crash Is Coming (2020)* (Cambridge House International, 2018), https://www.youtube.com/watch?v=WD2zcyfwdJ4)

final piece of the Hegelian equation.

V

The United Nations' Agenda 21/2030: The Rise of the American Technocracy

"I just wonder what it would be like to be reincarnated in an animal whose species had been so reduced in numbers than it was in danger of extinction. What would be its feelings toward the human species whose population explosion had denied it somewhere to exist... I must confess that I am tempted to ask for reincarnation as a particularly deadly virus."

Prince Phillip in Foreword for If I Were an Animal by Fleur Cowles, 1987

The increasing size of government directly results from the widespread adoption of the precautionary principle among the nation's scholars, politicians, and bureaucrats. They are all addicted to a "regulate-everything" mentality. America's increased reliance on technical specialists and regulators is not an accident. It is the direct result of infiltration by outside actors who have a specific goal in mind with America's political structure. Formerly known as Agenda 21, the United Nations' Agenda 2030 is the perfect embodiment of the precautionary principle and its child, the "Green" or "Sustainable Development" movement. It is the structural enforcement of a regulatory agenda that aims to mitigate the consistent threat that mankind poses on the world's ecosystems. On its face, it sounds friendly, right? In reality, Agenda 2030 encompasses the current neoliberal and neoconservative mindsets that recommend all facets of human activity must be scrutinized and controlled. These political ideologies represent the destruction of individual liberty on a massive scale through financial manipulation, increased government regulation, and social engineering. This narrative aims to prove that the main objective of Agenda 2030 is to subvert the American Constitution and the American way of life that our Founders envisioned. It represents the ultimate encumbrance on individual rights, property rights, and economic rights. Its theories represent the main driver behind the pain and suffering many Americans are experiencing due to their inability to traverse the economic ladder as the country transitions into an economically and culturally depressed state. As more cities and states adopt the United Nations' Agenda 2030 policies, this suffering will only worsen.

To further understand this program and the possible repercussions of its implementation, we must first focus on the history of the sustainable development movement and then examine the legislation that Agenda 2030 proposes. Simultaneously, we must examine the special interests, forces of public influence, and all Federal agencies that have instituted Agenda 2030 programs. Overall, Agenda 2030 is the regulatory framework for a dystopian technocracy where all forms of human activity will be regulated and controlled under the guise of saving the planet. It represents the final piece in the global equation; the economic crisis in 2008 and the purported climate crisis represent the problems while Agenda 2030 will serve as the overall solution.

The history of the term and concept of "environmentalism" truly began during the Age of Enlightenment (1650-1700). Henry David Thoreau wrote in his book, *Maine Woods*, that he believed the sanctity of the environment and "virgin" forests must be protected. In America, the concept gained its roots through the works of President Theodore Roosevelt and his aim to popularize the idea of conservation. His ideas grabbed the American public's attention: after his tenure, the National Park system was created in 1916. In 1962, Rachel Carson published her book *Silent Spring* that examined the harmful consequences that pesticides and other unnatural chemicals could have on the world's ecological systems and the fact that they may cause cancer. Her book helped reinvigorate the environmentalist movement. Later, in the 1970s, a series of books and papers examined that private industries were not conducting business in an ecologically safe manner (i.e., the oil and nuclear power industries). Disasters at Love Canal in 1978 and the nuclear crisis of Chernobyl in 1979 only augmented the perceived need for government regulation. During this decade, there were a series of legislative proposals that successfully made its way through Congress and on to the law books: the National Environmental Policy Act, the Clean Air Act, the banning of DDT (a harmful pesticide), the Water Pollution Control Act, and the Endangered Species Act. Clearly, from the 19th century onward, the environmentalist agenda slowly made its way from the writings of philosophers like Thoreau to legislative action proposed through the institution of Congress in the 1970s. From this moment forward, new agreements and proposals would only strengthen this movement. Although many of these regulations had great intentions, it will be shown that they have had unintended consequences. Some activists are aware of these consequences, and some are not. Those that are, understand that they are trying to do more than simply protect the environment; they aim to change and alter certain aspects of society to uphold a specific, unrelated agenda.

In 1992, in Rio de Janeiro, Brazil, the United Nations held the Conference on Environment and Development, commonly known as the Earth Summit. All members of the UN attended, including 2400 nongovernmental organizations. On Prince Charles' private yacht, President George H.W. Bush signed on to the agreement proposed, called Agenda 21.[1] Ultimately, the goals of Agenda 2030 can be summarized with the objective listed on the United Nations' website:

> Governments recognize that there is a new global effort to relate the elements of the international economic system and mankind's need for a safe and stable natural environment. Therefore, it is the intent of Governments that consensus-building at the intersection of the environmental and trade and development areas will be ongoing international forums, as well as in the domestic policy of each country... An open, equitable, secure, non-discriminatory, and predictable multilateral trading system that is consistent with the goals of sustainable development and leads to the optimal distribution of global production....[2]

The document continues to state the overall mentality that they aim to encourage among everyday citizens and national governments alike:

1. To promote patterns of consumption and production that reduce environmental stress and will meet the basic needs of humanity.

---

[1] Poole, Stephen. "Benefit Corporations: Expansion of the Public-Private Fascist State, Part 4." *Freedom Advocates | Exposing Agenda 21 and Sustainable Development.* (Freedom Advocates), 17 Aug. 2011. Accessed December 1, 2011, http://www.freedomadvocates.org/articles/illegitimate_government/benefit_corporations:_expansion_of_the_public-private_fascist_state,_part_4_20110817449)

[2] "Agenda 21" (United Nations, 1992), https://sustainabledevelopment.un.org/content/documents/Agenda21.pdf, Ch.2)

2. To develop a better understanding of the role of consumption and how to bring about more sustainable consumption patterns.[3]

The primary purpose of Agenda 21 is to create a new currency that reflects the economic and environmental needs of all countries and their people. "A multilateral trading system" is a new type of currency. The objectives also focus on economic planning under the premise that the surrounding environment's health requires it. A new, ulterior motive reveals itself: The United Nations is creating a new economic monopoly on human ecological output. Citizens will be taxed for merely existing!

Agenda 2030 is an expansion on the ideas that make up Agenda 21. Without a doubt, it provides the flowery language necessary to sell this new economic and political environment to the world:

> We envisage a world free of poverty, hunger, disease and want, where all life can thrive. We envisage a world free of fear and violence.
> A world with universal literacy. A world with equitable and universal access to
> quality education at all levels, to health care and social protection, where physical,
> mental and social well-being are assured. A world where we reaffirm our commitments regarding the human right to safe drinking water and sanitation and where there is improved hygiene; and where food is sufficient, safe, affordable and nutritious. A world where human habitats are safe, resilient and sustainable and where there is universal access to affordable, reliable and sustainable energy.[4]

In the United Nations' view, governments must find ways to promote sustainable consumption and production patterns that maintain the essential needs of mankind and the natural environment, or else all ecological systems will fail. An obvious conflict of interest, they also want a new currency to trade with and make bets on to ensure that this all happens.

The argument is clear: for the world to survive, man-

3 "Agenda 21" (United Nations, 1992), https://sustainabledevelopment.un.org/content/documents/Agenda21.pdf, Ch.4)

4 "Transforming Our World: the 2030 Agenda for Sustainable Development," United Nations (United Nations), accessed March 1, 2020, https://sustainabledevelopment.un.org/post2015/transformingourworld)

kind must drastically change and restrain their behavior. The young and fiery Democratic Congresswoman from New York, Alexandria Ocasio-Cortez, recently stated that "the world is going to end in 12 years if we don't address climate change."[5] What better way to promote a new regulatory environment by threatening mankind with the end of the world if it is not instituted? It is not a coincidence that Ocasio-Cortez's 12-year timeline lines up precisely with the United Nations' Agenda 2030 plan.

The machinations to successfully implement this structure are very complex and widespread. These regulatory bodies must aim to resolve the world's hunger crisis, economic instability, natural resource instability, and the supposed man-made climate change crisis that plagues our planet. By and large, Agenda 2030's intricate and lengthy proposal aims to regulate every human activity under the guise of reducing one's "carbon footprint." In the United Nations' view, there must be accountability regarding chemical use, natural resource allocation, land allocation, human population allocation, waste allocation, and regulation of all industries that may undermine sustainable development for the world.[6] The UN Agenda 2030 thesis states that their main objective is to:

> Improve progressively, through 2030, global resource efficiency in consumption and production and endeavour to decouple economic growth from environmental degradation, in accordance with the 10-Year Framework of Programmes on Sustainable Consumption and Production, with developed countries taking the lead.[7]

Their thesis asserts that these areas must be regulated to prevent stratospheric ozone depletion, transboundary atmospheric pollution, and the general problem of contamination in ecologically important areas.[8] When one examines the goals further, it is clear that the majority of these recommendations focus on the move-

5 Tim Hains, "Ocasio-Cortez: 'The World Is Going To End In 12 Years If We Don't Address Climate Change,'" RealClearPolitics, January 22, 2019, https://www.realclearpolitics.com/video/2019/01/22/ocasio-cortez_the_world_is_going_to_end_in_12_years_if_we_dont_address_climate_change.html)

6 "Agenda 21" (United Nations, 1992), https://sustainabledevelopment.un.org/content/documents/Agenda21.pdf)

7 "Transforming Our World: the 2030 Agenda for Sustainable Development," United Nations (United Nations), accessed March 1, 2020, https://sustainabledevelopment.un.org/post2015/transformingourworld)

8 "Agenda 21" (United Nations, 1992), https://sustainabledevelopment.un.org/content/documents/Agenda21.pdf, Ch. 7)

ment of people, how they live, and where they should reside.

When President George H.W. Bush signed on to the Agenda 21 proposal in 1992, he had done so without congressional approval. Almost every legislative process regarding this document has circumvented the United States Constitution's framework through the process of the executive order, effectively bypassing Congress and the American people. On June 29th, 1993, President Bill Clinton signed Executive Order 12852, which created the President's Council on Sustainable Development.[9] More recently, on June 9th, 2011, Barack Obama signed Executive Order 13575, which directly reflects the policies of Agenda 21 and Agenda 2030.[10] Because this movement has grown on an exponential basis, it has permeated through every level of government. Any government official who questions "going green" will be crucified by fabricated "popular public opinion" from the mainstream media and the scientists who help push the big lie.

The average citizen would be hard-pressed not to find documents, legislation, or other proposals directly related to sustainable development and Agenda 2030 within their local governments. Yes, UN proposals have avoided the rule of law through Executive Orders, and they have violated the United States Constitution. Furthermore, the organizations surrounding Agenda 2030 have avoided using Federal means to implement their procedures----many of these new regulations have been initiated at the local level (city governments) with the help of nongovernmental organizations from the ground-up. However, with the plethora of legislation relating to sustainable development that has followed our Constitution through the institution of the Congress, it would be deceitful to claim that the environmentalist agenda has completely ignored all of our governmental procedures. It is popular to care about the environment, and the UN planners behind Agenda 2030 have tactfully attached their financial and political goals with those of the environmental movement. Agenda 2030 is a well-funded policy initiative implemented at every level to secure a new social and economic

[9] "Executive Order 12852-Presidents Council on Sustainable Development," Executive Order 12852-Presidents Council on Sustainable Development | *The American Presidency Project*, June 29, 1993, http://www.presidency.ucsb.edu/ws/index.php?pid=61547)

[10] Exec. Order No. 13575, 3 CFR (2011).

order, creating multiple constitutional and legal crises in the process.

Nongovernmental organizations (NGOs)

Agenda 2030 has fervently expressed that nongovernmental organizations are essential to the implementation of these policies. Over 2400 nongovernmental organizations attended the original Earth Summit in 1992. One of the leading organizations, ICLEI (International Council for Local Environmental Initiatives), has been a strong advocate for implementing sustainable development policies at the local level. ICLEI was founded in 1990 when more than 200 local governments from 43 different countries convened for the World Congress of Local Governments for a Sustainable Future at the United Nations.[11] Today, ICLEI consistently receives large grants from the Rockefeller Brothers Fund, a foundation created by the prestigious Rockefeller family.[12] Another staple in the sustainable development community is the Carnegie Institution of Science, founded by Andrew Carnegie in 1895.[13] Many of these groups are placed strategically throughout the United States, such as the Sustainable Development Strategies Group, located in Gunnison, Colorado.[14] In every state, there are many groups similar to that of SDSG. One of the most influential contributors to Agenda 2030 is the Wildlands Network (formerly known as the Wildlands Project).[15] This group has direct input into land allocation and wildlife protection. There are thousands of groups who contribute financial and academic resources consistently to sustainable development policy implementation.

[11] *ICLEI - Local Governments for Sustainability: Homepage.* International Council of Local Environmental Initiatives, 1995. (ICLEI) Accessed December 11, 2011. (http://www.iclei.org)

[12] "Asian Cities Climate Change Resilience Network (ACCCRN): The Rockefeller Foundation." *The Rockefeller Foundation.* (The Rockefeller Foundation) Accessed December 11, 2011. (http://www.rockefellerfoundation.org/what-we-do/current-work/developing-climate-change-resilience/acccrn-partners)

[13] *Carnegie Institution for Science | Homepage.* (Carnegie Institution for Science) Accessed December 11, 2011. (http://carnegiescience.edu/)

[14] "About Us." *SDSG.* (Sustainable Development Strategies Group) Accessed December 11, 2011. (http://www.sdsg.org/about-us/)

[15] Wildlands Network. *(Wildlands Network) Accessed December 11, 2011. (http://www.twp.org/)*

Engagement from Local Government

The size and scope of these programs can be found on the national level, the state level, and the local level. With coordination at the local level from non- governmental organizations, Executive Orders from multiple Presidents, and legislation from Congress, the sustainable development agenda represents a fully comprehensive approach for restructuring the American government and eventually the world. The United Nations has always asserted that the Agenda 2030 sustainable development program will only be successful when its recommendations are implemented at the lower levels of government first:

> Activities that will contribute to the integrated promotion of sustainable livelihoods and environmental protection cover various sectoral interventions involving a range of actors, from local to global, and are essential at every level, especially the community and local levels.[16]

The entire proposal argues that local regulatory bodies must adhere to Agenda 2030 protocols to be successful. Or, in their words, "for mankind to be able to survive."

Engagement from the Federal Government

Just about every government agency has been handed the task of promoting the sustainable development agenda. In President Barack Obama's Executive Order 13575, there are twenty-five bureaucracies and agencies that will implement the White House Rural Council's policies, developed to ensure that the goals of Agenda 2030 are met:

- Department of the Treasury
- Department of Defense
- Department of Justice
- Department of the Interior
- Department of Commerce
- Department of Labor
- Department of Health and Human Services
- Department of Housing and Urban Development
- Department of Transportation

[16] "Agenda 21" (United Nations, 1992), https://sustainabledevelopment.un.org/content/documents/Agenda21.pdf, Chapter 3)

82

- Department of Energy
- Department of Education
- Department of Veterans Affairs
- Department of Homeland Security
- Environmental Protection Agency
- Federal Communications Commission
- Office of Management and Budget
- Office of Science and Technology Policy
- Office of National Drug Control Policy
- Council of Economic Advisers
- Domestic Policy Council
- National Economic Council
- Small Business Administration
- Council on Environmental Quality
- White House Office of Public Engagement and Intergovernmental Affairs
- White House Office of Cabinet Affairs.[17]

Without a doubt, all of these different bureaucracies' involvement demonstrates the efficiency of the Agenda 2030 program and other programs that support sustainable development initiatives. Executive Order 13575's central objective states:

> Sixteen percent of the American population lives in rural counties. Strong, **sustainable** rural communities are essential to winning the future and ensuring American competitiveness in the years ahead. These communities supply our food, fiber, and energy, safeguard our natural resources and are essential in the development of science and innovation. Though rural communities face numerous challenges, they also present enormous economic potential. The Federal Government has an important role to play in order to expand access to the capital necessary for economic growth, promote innovation, improve access to health care and education, and expand outdoor recreational **activities on public lands.**[18]

Simply stated, President Obama's executive order using flowery language about "healthcare, economic growth, and innovation" but leaves the real intention of the order hidden in plain sight.

---

[17] *Exec. Order No. 13575, 3 CFR (2011).*

[18] Ibid.

The executive order's primary emphasis is to expand the federal government's role on public and rural lands to increase their land acquisitions to reduce human activity in these areas. For areas that must exist, they must be connected to "the grid." This plan is directly in line with Agenda 2030's goal to restrict access to private ownership.

All of us must recognize that legislation that could drastically change one's life must be inspected thoroughly. Many questions arise out of Agenda 2030's proposition. It is vital that all personal and national relationships surrounding Agenda 2030's creation be examined. Simultaneously, it is essential to examine further the questionable instruments used for Agenda 2030's realization. These ideas pose a severe risk to personal and national sovereignty----an American ideal that has always been held in the highest regard. It is also essential to analyze the overall costs of Agenda 2030's plan. Yet, the most critical aspect of Agenda 2030 that must be revisited is the idea that mankind is the sole perpetrator of the world's supposed destruction. Will these assessments further stabilize the overall argument for the implementation of the United Nations' Agenda 2030? Or, is it a deceitful conspiracy to institute a form of government that no citizen would ever want to imagine?

To understand the real objectives of Agenda 2030, we must look at the perspectives and motivations of those who support it. The financial support of organizations that support Agenda 2030 from the likes of the Carnegie and Rockefeller families creates an irrefutable credibility problem. When words of Agenda 2030 are combined with the ideologies supported by these two families, it paints a frightening picture. Agenda 2030 consistently mentions its support of population control: "An assessment should also be made of [the] national population carrying capacity in the context of satisfaction of human needs and sustainable development...."[19] It is documented that both Andrew Carnegie and John D. Rockefeller financed millions of dollars to organizations that advocate the principles of eugenics in the late 19th and early 20th centuries. Both of these men and their institutions supported the same scientists who performed mass genocide at concentration camps like Auschwitz in Nazi

[19] "Agenda 21" (United Nations, 1992), https://sustainabledevelopment.un.org/content/documents/Agenda21.pdf, Chapter 5)

84

Germany.[20] These institutions and their ancestors' motivations have not changed; they are still funding the same policy agendas.

Former National Security Advisor and futurist Zbigniew Brzezinski describes the technocratic elite's position in his book, *Between Two Ages*. Many of Brzezinski's assertions regarding new computer technology and its impact on society are accurate. Brzezinski's analysis focuses mainly on society's transition from an industrial-based economy to a service-based economy rooted in technology:

> The post-industrial society is becoming a "technetronic" society—a society that is shaped culturally, psychologically, socially, and economically by the impact of technology and electronics — particularly in the area of computers and communications. The industrial process is no longer the principal determinant of social change, altering the mores, the social structure, and the values of society.[21]

The technetronic society that Brzezinski envisions will transform the relationship between individuals and the nation-state they belong to:

> ...just as the shift from an agrarian economy and feudal politics toward an industrial society and political systems based on the individual's emotional identification with the nation-state gave rise to contemporary international politics, so the appearance of the technetronic society reflects the onset of a new relationship between man and his *expanded global reality.*[22]

The "global reality" that he refers to is personified in the United Nations' Agenda 2030 proposal.

Brzezinski felt that although new computer technology would paradoxically create unity and division across the world at the same time, he contends that "a global human conscience is for the first time beginning to manifest itself."[23] He recognizes that the industrial age was linked to what we know as

[20] Black, Edwin. "The Horrifying American Roots of Nazi Eugenics." *History News Network*. George Mason University, 25 Nov. 2003. (History News Network) Accessed December 11, 2011. (http://hnn.us/articles/1796.html)

[21] Zbigniew Brzezinski, *Between Two Ages: Americas Role in the Technetronic Era* (Westport, CT: Greenwood Press, 1982), 10.)

[22] Ibid. 11.

[23] Ibid. p. 28.

modern contemporary international politics, where individual nation-states hold on to their sovereignty and negotiate with each other on an individual basis. Largely, *Between Two Ages* represents a plan to absorb the technological revolution for a new global form of government. During the technetronic era, the concept of the nation-state must be sacrificed for mankind to thrive. All of this directly relates to the goals of Agenda 2030 as electronic computer technology is dependent on the energy industries and the bureaucracies that regulate them. Likewise, Agenda 2030 is dependent on technology for its administration. Sustainable development and quantum computer analysis are not mutually exclusive; they are mutually codependent for one another.

Moving forward to the modern era, one man leading the technological revolution in America is Elon Musk, CEO of Tesla. Most Americans view Elon as a quirky genius who likes to smoke pot on the Joe Rogan podcast. Musk and Tesla are much more than a company that bills itself as an electric car company purely focused on sustainability. Tesla has been heavily subsidized by the federal government and is therefore heavily reliant on these subsidies for its success. His business model is directly in line with the UN 2030 Agenda for Sustainable Development, so he is receiving strong support from the Federal government. Although its corporate stock has skyrocketed since going public, it has yet to prove it can survive on its own in the supposedly free American market. When examining Musk's career, it is clear that he has been hand-selected by the elite to propel their agenda forward. Along with the government subsidies, he has been awarded several government contracts, such as a $645 Million deal with SpaceX and the US Air Force to fly GPS and earth-imaging satellites.[24] Musk claims to be an ally of humanity with his space technology advancements with SpaceX and new transportation projects completed by Tesla. On the one hand, he contends that artificial intelligence is the greatest threat to humanity. In the same breath, he contends that it is an inevitable creation, and someone with a philosopher-king mentality must lead the revolution:

the biggest mistake that I see artificial intelligence re-

[24] Tim Fernholz, "SpaceX Wins Lucrative New Contracts to Fly GPS and Earth-Imaging Satellites," Quartz (Quartz, March 15, 2018), https://qz.com/1229463/elon-musks-spacex-wins-lucrative-new-contracts-to-fly-gps-and-earth-imaging-satellites-for-the-us-air-force/)

searchers making is assuming that they're intelligent. Yeah they're not, compared to AI… AI will be vastly smarter—vastly. So what do you do with a situation like that? …you know, the old saying, if you can't beat them, join them. You know, that's what Neuralink is about. Can we be able to go along for the ride with AI? I really think that there should be other companies like Neuralink, essentially, to create a high bandwidth interface to the brain. Because right now, we are already a cyborg.[25]

Musk's grandfather and fellow technocrat, Dr. Joshua Haldeman, would be proud. Haldeman was a well-known economist and politician who led the Technocracy, Inc. political organization in Canada from 1936 to 1941. The Canadian authorities charged the organization for being aligned with socialist and fascist movements in Europe and ordered the organization to be disbanded.[26] Without a doubt, Musk's family history and status as a technocrat genius in America put him at the forefront of the movement Brzezinski and others are pushing forward.

Other well-known financiers have raised similar concerns about over-population. In 1997, Ted Turner funded over one billion dollars to organizations that promote Agenda 2030.[27] Previously, in 1996, Ted Turner stated in an interview with Audubon environmental magazine that "a total population of 250-300 million people, a 95% decline from present levels, would be ideal."[28] Later, in February of 2010, another prominent financier of sustainable development, Bill Gates, spoke at the TED conference about his ideas for saving humanity: "The world today has 6.8 billion people. That's heading up to about nine billion. Now if we do a really great job on new vaccines, health care, reproductive health services, we could lower that by

25 Ricki Harris, "Elon Musk: Humanity Is a Kind of 'Biological Boot Loader' for AI," Wired (Conde Nast, n.d.), https://www.wired.com/story/elon-musk-humanity-biological-boot-loader-ai/)

26 Joseph C Keating and Scott Haldeman, "Joshua N Haldeman, DC: the Canadian Years, 1926-1950," The Journal of the Canadian Chiropractic Association, September 1995, pp. 172-186, https://www.ncbi.nlm.nih.gov/pmc/articles/PMC2485067/pdf/jcca00035-0046.pdf)

27 Krasno, Jean E. The United Nations: Confronting the Challenges of a Global Society. (Lynne Rienner, 2004), p. 303)

28 "Depopulation Quotes." The Sovereign Independent. (The Sovereign Independent) Accessed December 11, 2011. (http://www.sovereignindependent.com/?p=2574)

perhaps 10 or 15 percent!"[29] After reading these statements, it is only logical to assume that Agenda 2030 is directly connected to these objectives. How do Mr. Turner and others like him propose reducing the population to these "ideal" levels? Statements made by key financiers of Agenda 2030 have raised fears about the true intentions of this program.

To understand the full impact of sustainable development policies, we must examine the proposed regulatory environment. As the UN objectives stated, the scope of enforcement must encapsulate all areas where human activity is present, namely: all-natural resource management, land/property management, transportation, residential and industrial utility management, human consumption, and production pattern management. All areas of the human biosphere will be controlled and regulated.

Land Management and Property Rights

The participation of organizations like the Wildlands Network and the Federal Government's Bureau of Land Management may be the most controversial aspect of Agenda 2030. The Wildlands Network's main objective is to promote environmental sustainability throughout North America's remaining forest lands. Most of their policy proposals focus on the inevitable impact humans can have on the environment. They also study the forest's biosphere, examining the existence of different species and how and where they exist. The Bureau of Land Management is similar—they also focus on the enforcement of practical forest management and the protection of wildlife. These goals are synonymous with the ambitions of Agenda 2030. It is the perfect backdrop for increased government influence in areas that were previously untouched. Ultimately, it puts mankind at odds with its environment—like a virus—instead of part of its environment in a symbiotic relationship. Their proposals directly threaten the concept of private property. Agenda 2030 states: "As appropriate, they [world nations] should also concentrate on activities aimed at facilitating the transition from rural to urban lifestyles and

[29] *Bill Gates on Energy: Innovating to Zero!* | Video on TED.com. Perf. Bill Gates. TED: Ideas worth Spreading. (TED, Feb. 2010.) Accessed December 11, 2011. (http://www.ted.com/talks/bill_gates.html)

settlement patterns…"[30] Essentially, it continues to profess that to maintain natural habitats, mankind must be placed into "walkable communities."[31] In other words, skyscrapers, apartment complexes will eventually replace rural neighborhoods, and the concept of private property will consequently fade away. When these facts are combined with the Federal land ownership map, our current lifestyle's future-outlook appears grim **(over 50% of America's land will be hands-off for humans)**.

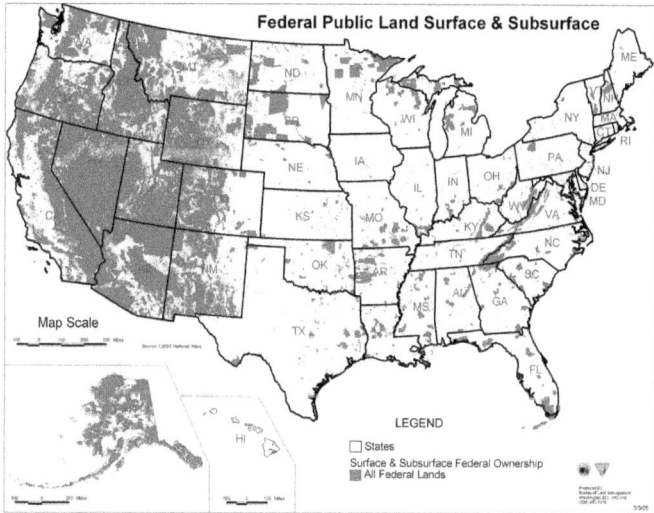

Figure (A) Federal Land Ownership Map, Bureau of Land Management.

Overall, these plans threaten the entire American way of life. Agenda 2030 will dictate where we live and whether we will ever be able to own private property. It is at this point that the endgame for the United Nations' Agenda 2030 plan becomes clear. Karl Marx, a self-proclaimed communist, states his views on private property in his book, *The Communist Manifesto*: "…

---

[30] "Agenda 21" (United Nations, 1992), https://sustainabledevelopment.un.org/content/documents/
Agenda21.pdf)

[31] Walkable and Livable Communities Institute Homepage. (Walklive) Accessed December 11, 2011.
(http://www.walklive.org/)

the theory of Communists may be summed up in the single sentence: Abolition of private property."[32] Do these words represent the principal ideals that have made America so great? The answer is an unequivocal no. Agenda 2030's policies directly reflect the policies proposed by Karl Marx. Eventually, all Wildlands will be barred from the settlement from humans. Visiting America's forests will continue to feel like a trip to Six Flags, with increasing park fees and restrictions. National parks and state parks have always coexisted with private land ownership. Under Agenda 2030, this relationship will no longer exist.

The best example of the expansion in government power over land rights is undeniably the Bundy Ranch situation in Nevada and the Oregon Standoff in 2016 that led to a direct violent conflict with the Federal government and resulted in the death of Robert Lavoy Finicum, a land rights activist. Both families contend that Federal government overreach has risen to dangerous levels and must be confronted. Cliven Bundy is a Nevada rancher who argues that the grazing fees, regulations, and land grabs imposed by the Bureau of Land Management have ruined his family's ranch and have stolen his property rights. He was mainly upset that the BLM had essentially restricted grazing access on 500,000 acres of the Bunkerville Allotment to protect the Desert Tortoise.[33] In effect, they had essentially stolen his livelihood for the protection of an animal. When his family originally purchased the land in the mid-1800s, he was granted grazing rights on the surrounding state public lands. During the standoff, the Bureau of Land Management confronted the family in an armed raid and also killed many of their livestock, which is pretty ironic considering this conflict was over the protection of a specific animal species.[34] Bundy attempted to pay the grazing fees in the early '90s, to Clark county, instead of the Federal government. It was clear that Bundy was okay with paying the fees, as long as his land rights were protected. In the end, the Federal

[32] Marx, Karl, Friedrich Engels, and E. J. Hobsbawm. *The Communist Manifesto: a Modern Edition.* (London: Verso, 1998), Chapter 1)

[33] Chris Kudialis, "Why Cliven Bundy Tried to Pay Grazing Fees to Clark County, Not BLM," Las Vegas Sun, November 07, 2017. (Las Vegas Sun) Accessed June 15, 2019. (https://lasvegassun.com/news/2017/nov/07/why-cliven-bundy-sent-grazing-fees-clark-county/)

[34] "EXCLUSIVE: Evidence of BLM's Deadly Abuse of Animals Taken from Bundy Ranch," 21st Century Wire, April 22, 2014. (21st Century Wire) Accessed June 15, 2019. (https://21stcenturywire.com/2014/04/16/exclusive-evidence-of-blms-deadly-abuse-of-animals-taken-from-bundy-ranch/)

government lost the case against Cliven and his family members for withholding evidence, while 19 others still face other related charges.[35] The land disputes themselves, however, will undoubtedly continue.

In a similar case, Oregon's situation unfolded after Dwight and Steven Hammond were charged with felony arson for burning forest slash on their property. The situation was the last straw for the Hammonds, who had a long list of other land rights' grievances against the Federal government. The BLM has increased its efforts in the name of environmentalism to restrict or invalidate certain rights on land or confiscate the land altogether. The Hammond family reacted by organizing among other land rights activists and taking over a federal building at a local wildlife refuge to state their cause. The occupation resulted in the brutal murder of Robert Lavoy Finicum, an activist from Arizona who was on his way with his family to meet other patriots and the local sheriff at the refuge center. Lavoy was shot by local police and federal agents with his hands in the air outside of his truck, directly in front of his entire family, who was luckily uninjured in the melee.

Nationwide, people are forced to bend to the will of local city councils who write erroneous zoning regulations that are there to force false scarcity into the market. With unnecessary and oppressive square footage requirements that limit the size of the home you can build, to whether or not you can utilize the backyard for gardening, one could argue that city councils and home owner's associations sometimes have more power than the state government. Erroneous price controls are placed on private single-family home purchases under the guise of "affordable housing," so that you can lose out on the gain in property value years later. There are numerous examples of negative consequences of government involvement in the market, whether intentional or unintentional.

Through and through, all of these programs' goal is to force people from rural communities into large urban centers where the economic and political elite can maintain a legalized

<hr>

[35] Robert Anglen, "Cliven Bundy Is Free, but Standoff Case Isn't Over: What You Need to Know," Azcentral, February 08, 2018. (AZ Central) Accessed June 15, 2019. (https://www.azcentral.com/story/news/local/arizona-investigations/2018/01/04/cliven-ammon-bundy-ranch-standoff-trial-what-know-nevada-ranching-mistrial/997221001/)

monopoly over the citizenry. By scaring people into thinking that humans destroy everything wherever they reside, the sheep will flock to large cities because government regulations have either forced them off of their land or moved their job to the city. Many will happily give up things like private land ownership, for convenience, social status, and financial security.

Housing and Construction

Of course, humans do not only use fossil fuels for their transportation needs. Housing also relies heavily on fossil fuels as they are needed to: build the home with necessary materials, heat and cool the home, and maintain the home. For these reasons, the construction industry is arguably one of the most heavily regulated sectors of the market. It also happens to be the industry that has a direct relationship with property ownership and its development, which falls under the scope of control of Agenda 2030 and its local counterparts.

The Council of Economic Advisers to President Trump issued a report in September 2019 entitled "The State of Homelessness in America." This report found that as the number of regulations increase, so do the costs.[36] Of these, the report found the following mandates to be the most burdensome on the housing market:

- overly restrictive zoning and growth management controls
- rent controls
- cumbersome building and rehabilitation codes
- excessive energy and water efficiency mandates
- unreasonable maximum-density allowances
- historic preservation requirements
- overly burdensome wetland or environmental regulations
- outdated manufactured-housing regulations and restrictions
- undue parking requirements
- cumbersome and time-consuming permitting and review

---

[36] "The State of Homelessness in America," The State of Homelessness in America § (2019), https://www.whitehouse.gov/wp-content/uploads/2019/09/The-State-of-Homelessness-in-America.pdf, p.13)

procedures
- tax policies that discourage investment or reinvestment
- overly complex labor requirements
- and inordinate impact or developer fees

Regulations are recommended by the Environmental Protection Agency and the International Code Council and then adopted by localities throughout the United States. These institutions have had a tremendous impact on the housing industry with their regulations; some understandably exist while others are extraordinary.

Many of these regulations were passed under the guidance from proponents of the UN Agenda 2030 program. The relationship between bureaucrat, land developer, home builder, and the consumer should be a cooperative one. In the last 40 years, it appears that the consumer has been kept out of the conversation on home building regulations. For example, the 2018 update for the International Energy Conservation Code specifically requires that 90% of the lighting in every home be wired only for high-efficacy lamps.[37] The current regulatory environment has had a significant impact on consumer choice—good and bad. On the one hand, it has forced manufacturers to develop creative lighting alternatives for homeowners. Many of the new LED bulbs have no problem mimicking the classic light bulb's effects—they are dimmable, have adjustable hues, and more. On the other hand, for the consumer that still appreciates the classic style of light bulb or is going for a specific look in their home, this regulation restricts their choices. Both technologies have their advantages, and the consumer should be the ultimate judge as to what goes in their home, especially as it relates to amenities.

Many of the things people see as necessary regulations (necessary insulation requirements, etc.) are selling points for builders. In other words, they are already incentivized to build a well-built home for the effects of the environment. Multiple studies have shown that LEED-Certified buildings are often less

[37] "Residential Provisions of the 2018 International Energy Conservation Code," Residential Provisions of the 2018 International Energy Conservation Code § (2018), https://www.energycodes.gov/sites/default/files/becu/2018_IECC_residential.pdf, p.19)

energy-efficient than their non-certified competitors.[38] In 2014, the Washington Examiner found that every LEED-registered building in Washington, DC, was the city's least energy-efficient buildings.[39] Many consumers have no problem choosing to be eco-friendly; it keeps money in their wallets in many circumstances. A government-issued "stamp of approval" often induces a lack of commitment to higher standards than those who want to sell a decent product.

The National Association of Home Builders reported in 2018 that government regulations account for 30% of today's multifamily home production costs nationwide.[40] The report from President Trump's economic council found that housing regulations, construction and development costs, housing prices, and the rate of homelessness all have direct relationships with one another. The data shows that cities with the most regulations also have the highest production costs, housing prices, and homeless populations. For cities with an average value-to-cost ratio of over 1.5, the percentage of homeless per 10,000 people ranged from 20-50%. For cities with lower value to cost ratios, homeless rates range from 10-30%.[41] The report concludes, "…if housing regulations do not constrain the supply of housing, then home values should not exceed the cost to produce a home. After all, in a housing market without supply constraints, new homes would be built until home values fell to their production cost."[42] The correlations seen within the data paint an obvious picture of a poorly structured housing market.

Without a doubt, to build a home in today's regulatory environment, you need a decent amount of capital to do so.

[38] Capital Flows, "LEED-Certified Buildings Are Often Less Energy-Efficient Than Uncertified Ones," Forbes (Forbes Magazine, May 1, 2014), https://www.forbes.com/sites/realspin/2014/04/30/leed-certified-buildings-are-often-less-energy-efficient-than-uncertified-ones/#3bdb4f125544)

[39] Luke Rosiak and Richard Pollock, "EXography: Worst-of-the-Worst in Energy Efficiency Earn LEED's Highest --- and Meaningless --- Rating," Washington Examiner, January 14, 2014, https://www.washingtonexaminer.com/exography-worst-of-the-worst-in-energy-efficiency-earn-leeds-highest-and-meaningless-rating)

[40] Paul Emrath and Caitlin Walter, "Regulation: Over 30 Percent of the Cost of a Multifamily Development," NAHB (National Association of Home Builders, June 12, 2018), https://www.nahbclassic.org/generic.aspx?genericContentID=262391)

[41] "The State of Homelessness in America," The State of Homelessness in America § (2019), https://www.whitehouse.gov/wp-content/uploads/2019/09/The-State-of-Homelessness-in-America.pdf, p.13)

[42] Ibid.

The UN environmental agenda has negatively impacted home-ownership in America. If you are lucky enough to own a home, being creative with your home is limited due to the burdensome permitting processes in every major U.S. city. The stated goals of Agenda 2030 have had a direct impact on the nuances of property ownership and the ability to own a home.

Transportation

Another function of Agenda 2030 is the regulatory environment surrounding the movement of human populations. Seeing as carbon represents the ultimate villain among climate change "experts," transportation regulations have become increasingly powerful and broad in scope. The main objective of Agenda 2030 is to get people out of cars they own into mass transit systems to decrease their "carbon footprint" and simultaneously control their movement. Instead of presenting a comprehensive approach where all options are offered, sustainable development proponents are waging war on those who enjoy their autonomy. Owning a car provides too much freedom, which will result in people traveling on lands that humans should not be visiting, as we destroy everything we touch. Urban sprawl must be stopped, they say.

To further illustrate this fact, it is necessary to examine some of the proposed transportation regulations and programs by cities that have aligned themselves with the sustainable development movement. By increasing automobile manufacturing regulations with safety rules such as requiring back-up cameras or electronic blind spot detectors in all vehicles[43], the costs inevitably increase as the regulations do. Since 1975, the consumer price index for new vehicles has increased by 145 percent.[44] Scholars at the University of Indiana contend that new fuel-efficiency regulations have saved Americans enough money to make up for the difference over time.[45] However, in the same breath,

---

[43] US Congress, House, Cameron Gulbransen Kids Transportation Safety Act of 2007. (KT Safety Act of 2007) Act of 2007, 1216, 110th Cong., 2nd sess., introduced in House December 19, 2007, https://www.govinfo.gov/content/pkg/STATUTE-122/pdf/STATUTE-122-Pg639.pdf

[44] "CPI for All Urban Consumers, New Vehicles in US City Average," US Bureau of Labor Statistics (US Bureau of Labor Statistics), Accessed February 22, 2020, https://data.bls.gov/pdq/SurveyOutputServlet)

[45] Sanya Carley et al., "A Macroeconomic Study of Federal and State Automotive Regulations" (Indiana University, March 2017), https://oneill.indiana.edu/doc/research/working-groups/auto-report-032017.pdf)

the report notes that young Americans seeking driver's licenses has consistently declined since 1983 and that "for the retail consumer, purchasing a vehicle is a major investment of household income, second in size only to the decision to buy a house or condominium."[46]   Today's vehicles have more censors and computer power than ever before, and costs have subsequently risen to the point where many choose to either buy older vehicles or utilize driver applications like Uber or Lyft. There are also companies like "Car2Go" where you can simply rent an electric vehicle within the city where vehicles are parked in public spaces for the next driver.

Alternatively, the government could simply ban gas-powered vehicles altogether, which is a new policy initiative coming out of California. The City of San Francisco banned all vehicle traffic on its popular market street at the beginning of 2020.[47] This new environment is Agenda 2030's main goal for vehicle traffic; many other cities plan to adopt similar regulations. Instead of adding protected bike lanes in addition to existing traffic lanes, bike lanes are simply replacing them. Instead of fixing or adding more roads, legislators are focusing more attention on adding mass transit systems. Metropolitan planning organizations like *PlanCheyenne* have endorsed recommendations for walking more, all in the name of reducing carbon footprints.[48] Their development plans call for "complete streets," where all transportation modes have equal access to the road.[49] These policies will be implemented nationwide.

[46] Sanya Carley et al., "A Macroeconomic Study of Federal and State Automotive Regulations" (Indiana University, March 2017), https://oneill.indiana.edu/doc/research/working-groups/auto-report-032017.pdf)

[47] Carlton Reid, "San Francisco Bans Cars From Market Street 124 Years After Bicyclists Called For Primacy," Forbes (Forbes Magazine, January 26, 2020), https://www.forbes.com/sites/carltonreid/2020/01/26/san-francisco-bans-cars-from-market-street-124-years-after--bicyclists-called-for-primacy/#6afd40a25387)

[48] "Cheyenne Metropolitan Area Pedestrian Plan," Cheyenne MPO (Cheyenne Metropolitan Planning Organization , August 2010), https://www.plancheyenne.org/mpo-project/cheyenne-metropolitan-area-pedestrian-plan/)

[49] Stacy Lynne, "Plan Cheyenne Town Hall," Plan Cheyenne Town Hall, accessed March 1, 2020, https://www.youtube.com/watch?v=iEABMOFdqAc)

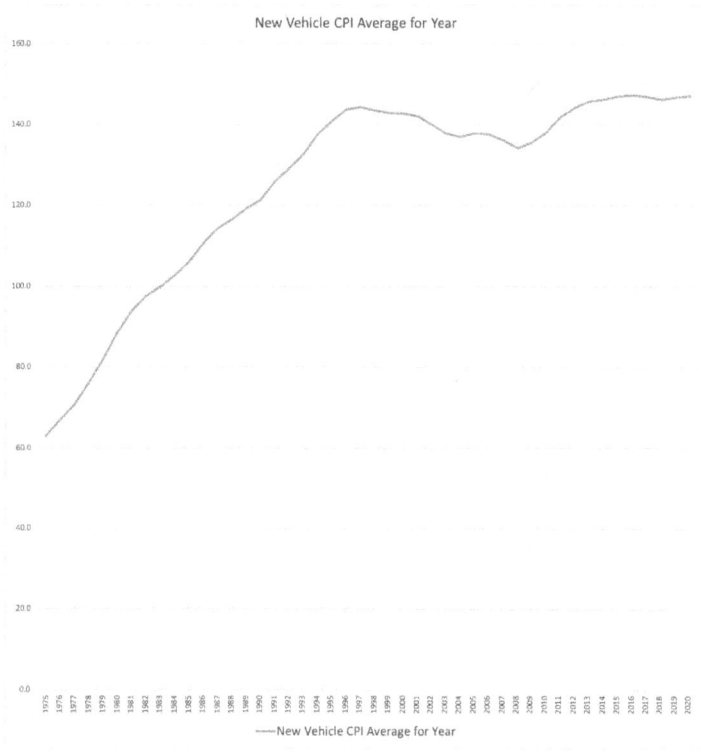

New Vehicle CPI Average for Year

——New Vehicle CPI Average for Year

Figure (B) New Vehicle Consumer Price Index, Bureau of Labor Statistics.

     If lanes are added, they are typically added to our high-way systems as toll roads with corrupt contracts that let multina-tional corporations earn profits while the residents foot the bill. In due time the entire road network in America will be connected electronically with 5G technology from corporations like Verizon and Panasonic. The connected superhighways that lead from Texas's southern tip and split off to the East and West coasts are all designed to be owned and operated by multinational corpora-tions. These corporations coordinate directly with governmental and nongovernmental organizations that support the United Nations' Agenda 2030.

97

Corrupt Multinational Toll Road Contracts

2004: Cintra (Spain) 50-year superhighway project for Trans-Texas Corridor connecting Mexico to the United States.[50]

2005: Cintra (Spain)/Macquarie Group (Australia) 99 year contract for Chicago Skyway.[51]

2005: Cintra (Spain) Indiana Toll Road[52]

2016: Mobility Partners (subsidiary of Cintra) 50 year contract with North Carolina DOT for I-77 Express Lanes.[53]

Agenda 2030 does not propose a comprehensive approach for transportation needs, where multiple options are offered. Instead, it recommends drastically reducing the carbon footprint, where citizens are forced to use mass transit, bike, or walk. The plan represents a form of social engineering, where the concept of free-choice is ignored and discarded. Most would agree that regardless of whether one believes in man-made global warming or not, pollution from vehicles with smog is not desirable. Nevertheless, we have to live on this planet and function as human beings, and it is not unreasonable to seek options that promote freedom of choice with incentives, rather than programs that seek to dictate a particular way of life. We must innovate, not dictate. All transportation options must be available in our cities.

Healthcare & COVID-19

The 2020 COVID-19 Pandemic is the final piece of the

[50] Daniel Gross, "Why Sell Toll Roads to Foreign Companies?" Slate Magazine, March 29, 2006, |PAGE|, accessed September 20, 2020, https://slate.com/business/2006/03/why-sell-toll-roads-to-foreign-companies.html)

[51] Nick Ochsner, "Toll Road Troubles: Politicians, Experts Point to Cintra's History as Cautionary Tale for NC," Https://www.wbtv.com, February 12, 2016, |PAGE|, accessed September 20, 2020, https://www.wbtv.com/story/31177025/toll-road-troubles-politicians-experts-point-to-cintras-history-as-cautionary-tale-for-nc/)

[52] Daniel Gross, "Why Sell Toll Roads to Foreign Companies?" Slate Magazine, March 29, 2006, accessed September 20, 2020, https://slate.com/business/2006/03/why-sell-toll-roads-to-foreign-companies.html)

[53] Nick Ochsner, "Toll Road Troubles: Politicians, Experts Point to Cintra's History as Cautionary Tale for NC," Https://www.wbtv.com, February 12, 2016, accessed September 20, 2020, https://www.wbtv.com/story/31177025/toll-road-troubles-politicians-experts-point-to-cintras-history-as-cautionary-tale-for-nc/)

Agenda 2030 structure. It represents the ultimate catalyst for the implementation of the program. The crux of Agenda 2030 is population control: control of land and housing, transportation, and personal autonomy. A deadly virus sweeping across the world is another crisis that cannot go to waste for global technocrats. The 2008 recession was the first phase of economic and political consolidation for the global elite. The final phase of this consolidation of power will be driven behind the fear that has permeated every crevice of the United States from the COVID-19 pandemic. After the COVID-19 chaos subsides, America and the world will never be the same.

The government intervention in the market in 2008 had only stalled the economic pain for a later time. The Federal Reserve has continued to print money and artificially lower interest rates to prop up the economy. After the COVID-19 virus took hold at the beginning of 2020, it revealed the US economy's false economic growth, which was built upon these artificial market interventions. The emperor has lost his clothes; Americans have awoken to the fact that their entire economy is based on a lie. Once again, a massive economic consolidation for the bankers and the technocratic elite is occurring; however, this time, it will be the final consolidation before a new economic and political system is implemented.

The Agenda 2030 program focuses on controlling land, people, and the movement of people. Luckily for the proponents of Agenda 2030, a viral pandemic is the perfect excuse to take control of these areas out of pure necessity. Immediately after the experts predicted a massive outbreak of the COVID-19 virus in the United States from China, President Trump locked the country down from the world. President Trump told us that "handshakes will be a thing of the past,"[54] and that the lockdown orders are necessary to protect the country and our way of life. State Governors and local municipalities ordered all businesses to be closed, with the only exception being predetermined "essential businesses." In essence, the entire country was under some form of martial law. Some states softly enforced the "stay-at-home orders," while others instituted a complete police state with the

[54] Paul Batura, "Paul Batura: Will Coronavirus Make Handshaking Go Extinct after Thousands of Years? Trump and Others Wonder," Fox News (FOX News Network, March 14, 2020), https://www.foxnews.com/opinion/coronavirus-alternatives-handshake-paul-batura)

national guard's help. California has gone as far as threatening to shut off the water and electricity to non-essential businesses who defy the order.[55] Every state has threatened citizens with arrest for not staying at home.

How will the world react moving forward? The shock that everyone has experienced from this event is meant to alter how we interact and transact with each other permanently. It will change how we communicate, how we do business, how we shop, how we travel, how we eat, how we exercise, and more. One year ago, we would scoff at mandated travel restrictions and business closures due to a virus. Many saw the possibility of a pandemic as something that only comes out of the writer's studios in Hollywood. Yet, it is real. Americans are scared. The world is scared. Ask any economist; fear is arguably the most powerful driver of any economy. This principle is no different when applied to a political canon.

Under COVID-19 restrictions, Americans have given up more freedom than any other time in US history since the Civil War. People are no longer allowed to congregate in groups of ten or more, which has resulted in religious institutions being shut down. A defiant pastor in New Orleans was arrested for violating this order.[56] Religious freedom under the First Amendment was immediately sacrificed for security and safety. Gun shops were also deemed non-essential by all state governors, and for those who were allowed to operate, state background check operations were backlogged for days resulting in delayed sales.[57] As many gun advocates say, "a right delayed is a right denied." Stay-at-home orders are now the law in most states, and anyone who violates this law will be arrested.[58] This law and other quarantine orders are clear violations of the Constitution's 4th Amendment,

[55] Sarah Parvini, "LA Threatens to Shut off Water, Power of Businesses Breaking Coronavirus Rules," Los Angeles Times (Los Angeles Times, March 25, 2020), https://www.latimes.com/california/story/2020-03-25/la-water-power-businesses-coronavirus-closure-rules)

[56] "Louisiana Pastor Arrested after Holding Services despite Stay-at-Home Order, Report Says," WWL (WWL, March 31, 2020), https://www.wwltv.com/article/news/health/coronavirus/louisiana-pastor-arrested-after-holding-services-despite-coronavirus-order-report-says/289-4394a314-3c13-4047-95d7-e4f65f517752)

[57] Michael Karlik, "Background Checks for Guns Triple as Wait Times Cross Federal Threshold," Colorado Politics, March 30, 2020, https://www.coloradopolitics.com/coronavirus/background-checks-for-guns-triple-as-wait-times-cross-federal-threshold/article_72d2a81c-6e0f-11ea-81d5-47623c7fe29a.html)

[58] "Governor Gavin Newsom Issues Stay at Home Order," California Governor, March 21, 2020, https://www.gov.ca.gov/2020/03/19/governor-gavin-newsom-issues-stay-at-home-order/)

which protects against illegal searches and seizures, and the 5th Amendment, which protects individuals from unnecessarily disclosing information, also known as the right to remain silent. There has been some resistance, but for the most part, Americans have willingly given up these freedoms under the premise that these infringements are only temporary in order to "flatten the curve." Is there ever an example of government pulling back the fence that they put on our yard? As they say, once you give a mouse a cookie, he wants a glass of milk to go with it.

The initial outbreak of COVID-19 occurred in Wuhan, China, a city with a well-known level 4 bio lab. As news of the virus outbreak and its severity was revealed to the world, accusations of malfeasance and a blatant cover-up of the infection data immediately followed. According to US intelligence sources, China has both under-reported the total number of cases and deaths.[59] Simultaneously, there have been just as many doctors, virologists, and other specialists that have alleged that the virus is man-made as there are that contend this virus occurred naturally. Researchers from the School of Biological Sciences for the Indian Institute of Technology and University of Delhi stated in their now-retracted report:

> The finding of 4 unique inserts in the 2019-nCoV, all of which have identity /similarity to amino acid residues in key structural proteins of HIV-1 is unlikely to be fortuitous in nature. This work provides yet unknown insights on 2019-nCoV and sheds light on the evolution and pathogenicity of this virus with important implications for diagnosis of this virus.[60]

Just after the Chinese President Xi Jinping discussed the urgent need to contain the virus, the Chinese Ministry of Science and Technology issued a new directive entitled: "Instructions on strengthening biosecurity management in microbiology labs that handle advanced viruses like the novel coronavirus." China also dispatched its top biological warfare expert, Major Chen

[59] Nick Wadhams and Jennifer Jacobs, "China Concealed Extent of Virus Outbreak, US Intelligence Says," Bloomberg.com (Bloomberg, April 1, 2020), https://www.bloomberg.com/news/articles/2020-04-01/china-concealed-extent-of-virus-outbreak-u-s-intelligence-says)

[60] Bishwajit Kundu, "Uncanny Similarity of Unique Inserts in the 2019-NCoV Spike Protein to HIV-1 gp120 and Gag "(BIORxRv, February 2, 2020), https://www.biorxiv.org/content/10.1101/2020.01.30.9278 71v1.full.pdf)

Wei, to Wuhan as the outbreak took hold.[61] Those that allege that COVID-19 is a man-made bioweapon should not be shouted down but acknowledged and accepted on the world's debate stage.

The most interesting aspect of the COVID-19 virus is not the outbreak itself, but the theories concerning a potential worldwide pandemic before the actual event. At first glance, it appears that these NGOs and think-tanks are merely planning for the worst. When one looks closer, there is no denying that there is too much to gain for these groups if a pandemic outbreak actually happens. The Rockefeller Foundation and now-defunct Global Business Network issued their report "Scenarios for the Future of Technology and International Development" in May of 2010. Peter Schwartz, the co-founder, and chairman of the Global Business Network, states in the report's foreword:

> We are at a moment in history that is full of opportunity. Technology is poised to transform the lives of millions of people throughout the world, especially those who have had little or no access to the tools that can deliver sustainable improvements for their families and communities. From farmers using mobile phones to buy and sell crops to doctors remotely monitoring and treating influenza outbreaks in rural villages, technology is rapidly becoming more and more integral to the pace and progress of development.[62]

Schwartz continues by illustrating the main benefits of the Rockefeller Foundation's use of scenario planning:

> The Rockefeller Foundation's use of scenario planning to explore technology and international development has been both inspired and ambitious. Throughout my 40-plus-year career as a scenario planner, I have worked with many of the world's
>
> leading companies, governments, foundations, and nonprofits… Scenario planning is a powerful tool precisely because the future is unpredictable and shaped by many interacting

61 Steven W. Mosher, "Opinion: Don't Buy China's Story: The Coronavirus May Have Leaked from a Lab," New York Post (New York Post, March 5, 2020), https://nypost.com/2020/02/22/dont-buy-chinas-story-the-coronavirus-may-have-leaked-from-a-lab/)

62 Peter Schwartz, "Scenarios for the Future of Technology and International Development" (Rockefeller Foundation , June 2010), https://www.rockefellerfoundation.org/news/publications/scenarios-future-technology, p.6)

variables.[63]

Schwartz feels that new technology is necessary to shape the unpredictable world we all live in. What scenarios does Schwartz feel are the most likely?

The "LOCK STEP" scenario envisions "a world of tighter top-down government control and more authoritarian leadership, with limited innovation and growing citizen push-back." The scenario envisions explicitly a deadly pandemic as the main driver for authoritative control:

> In 2012, the pandemic that the world had been anticipating for years finally hit. Unlike 2009's H1N1, this new influenza strain...was extremely virulent and deadly. Even the most pandemic-prepared nations were quickly overwhelmed when the virus streaked around the world, infecting nearly 20 percent of the global population and killing 8 million in just seven months...The pandemic also had a deadly effect on economies: international mobility of both people and goods screeched to a halt, debilitating industries like tourism and breaking global supply chains. Even locally, ordinarily bustling shops and office buildings sat empty for months, devoid of both employees and customers.[64]

What solutions does LOCK STEP offer for the chaos? The report heavily relies on smart-grid technology to stop viral pandemics:

> • Scanners using advanced functional magnetic resonance imaging (fMRI) technology become the norm at airports and other public areas to detect abnormal behavior that may indicate "antisocial intent."
> • In the aftermath of pandemic scares, smarter packaging for food and beverages is applied first by big companies and producers in a business-to-business environment, and then adopted for individual products and consumers.
> • New diagnostics are developed to detect communicable diseases. The application of health screening also changes; screening becomes a prerequisite for release from a hospital or prison, successfully slowing the spread of many diseases.
> • Tele-presence technologies respond to the demand for less expensive, lower bandwidth,

---

63 Ibid, p. 6.

64 Ibid, p. 18.

sophisticated communications systems for populations whose travel is restricted.

The LOCK STEP scenario paints a dystopic vision for the future with an all-powerful police state enforcing travel restrictions to protect from the supposed constant threat of contagions, whether real or exaggerated.

Immediately before the outbreak in Wuhan, China, the John Hopkins Center for Health Security, the World Economic Forum, and the Bill and Melinda Gates Foundation hosted Event 201, a "high-level pandemic exercise" entitled "Event 201" on October 18, 2019, in New York, NY. The exercise was conducted to "illustrate areas where public/private partnerships will be necessary during the response to a severe pandemic in order to diminish large-scale economic and societal consequences." Eerily enough, the Event 201 exercise specifically chose a novel coronavirus as its virus of choice for the scenario in which 65 million people would die.[65] The organization had to issue a press release to correct the record that they *did not* predict this virus, and their scenario does not relate to the current COVID-19 outbreak. Considering the stated ideals of Bill Gates and his theories concerning population control, the timing and nature of this forum is concerning, to say the least.

Although the organizers of Event 201 claim that their goal is to "diminish" societal consequences, the statement could not be further from the truth. A deadly pandemic will inevitably change how we interact as a society. Those who consistently claim to offer solutions to a global virus often are the same individuals looking to profit from the new checks and balances required in the name of public safety. The recommendations made in this report, and others clearly illustrate that a *new society* will replace the existing one that will be destroyed by a cataclysmic event, like COVID-19. Agenda 2030 specifically calls for direct control over people's movement and how people interact with each other. As Peter Schwartz stated in the Rockefeller report, the goal is for people to have access to the tools that can "deliver sustainable developments for their families and communities." What will their new society look like?

[65] "Event 201, a Pandemic Exercise to Illustrate Preparedness Efforts," Event 201 (Center for Health Security, January 25, 2020), http://www.centerforhealthsecurity.org/event201/)

The Rise of the American Technocracy

The main objective for Agenda 2030 is to transform nations and their economies to build a new social order which resembles an archaic feudalist structure that will be controlled by technocrats, global financiers, and mega-corporations. Eventually, major U.S. cities will resemble the scenes out of the movie "Blade Runner," where everyone is crammed into oppressive megacities with corporations that control everything with the permission of a powerful oligarchical dictatorship. One would only need to supplement Amazon CEO Jeff Bezos for the evil corporate dictator that sees the little guy as nothing but a replaceable drone. This plan is being sold as a trendy idea under the moniker "smart cities."

The underlying theme found throughout the stated objectives of the United Nations' Agenda 2030 is the goal of ridding the concept of individual property ownership from the public domain worldwide. It is undeniable that this goal parallels the stated goals of the communist party. This structure will work hand-in-hand with new technologies that are designed to disrupt how humans coexist with each other. Promoted as something that is trendy and cool with applications like Uber, Lyft, and Car-2Go, Americans are giving up on the idea of owning a car and the concept of ownership altogether. With services like Spotify, people do not even purchase their music anymore; they now prefer to stream it through a subscription service. Why? It is simple: cost. Property ownership is becoming a privilege for a select few. With rental services like Spotify, technology has disrupted the sector with increased convenience and a decrease in cost. Americans have swapped viewing property ownership as an admirable and obtainable goal for viewing it as a rare privilege or unnecessary burden. Many of America's youth seems to be rejecting this idea altogether for convenience.

Homeownership among millennials is significantly lower than Gen X and Baby Boomer generations; only 32% of millennials were homeowners in 2015 compared to 60% of Gen Xers and 75% of baby boomers.[66] Still, they have no idea that

---

[66] Jung Hyun Choi, Jun Zhu, and Laurie Goodman, "The State of Millennial Homeownership," Urban Institute, July 18, 2018, https://www.urban.org/urban-wire/state-millennial-homeownership)

this reality was all created by design. They see corrupt land deals for apartments instead of condos or townhomes, which promote individual ownership as a direct consequence of a corrupt, capitalistic society. On the contrary, it results from corrupt city leaders who are promoting a new socialist utopia where they control housing costs in a unified monopoly between developer and government. Developers own the apartments, and the government owns "affordable housing." Freedom of choice in the market is no longer an option. The large corporate developers and the government are now landlords. Leased on the trendy basis of maximum sustainability, "micro-apartments" are now replacing standard apartments.[67] Forget the standard 800 square foot 1-bedroom apartment; you can survive in a 450 square foot closet! Whether it is owning a home, a car, or even a phone—Americans are now renting these assets rather than holding title to them. We are now a nation of renters who are addicted to the technology that has enabled our enslavement.

If Agenda 2030 were to be implemented thirty years ago, it would be impossible. The modern innovations of the 21st century have changed that fact. The "internet of things" has drastically changed our lifestyles forever, and its impact will only expand in the future. Smart meters help utility companies tell the difference between a washing machine, an oven range, or a refrigerator while also monitoring overall electricity usage, all in the name of purportedly reducing one's carbon footprint.[68] The US Appeals Court ruled in 2018 that utility companies are collecting data and that this search is reasonable under the 4th Amendment of the Constitution.[69] Smart refrigerators now track your grocery purchases if you choose to order through the fridge door's touch-screen display. Smart TVs now track the applications you use and the movies and TV shows you watch. If it has the moniker "smart" in it, the device is likely tracking you in some form or another.

---

[67] Peter Kotecki, "54 Photos of New York City Microapartments Show How Tiny Living Can Be Glamorous - or Disappointing," Business Insider (Business Insider, December 26, 2018), https://www.businessinsider.com/photos-nyc-micro-apartments-2018-10#this-129-million-apartment-in-midtown-manhattan-is-starved-for-storage-but-it-includes-several-crafty-design-elements-like-a-hidden-pantry-6)

[68] Karl Bode, "Your Smart Electricity Meter Can Easily Spy On You, Court Ruling Warns," Vice (Vice, August 24, 2018), https://www.vice.com/en_us/article/j5n3pb/your-smart-electricity-meter-can-easily-spy-on-you-court-ruling-warns)

[69] Naperville Smart Meter Awareness v. City of Naperville. 900 F.3d 521, 524 (7th Circuit, 2018).

Outside of the home, cameras are on every traffic light with speed tracking and license plate readers. One legislative proposal in Oregon outlined a plan to tax citizens by the mile by tracking drivers with their cellphone GPS data.[70] Driverless vehicles have added a new element to transportation technology that will change how our roads operate forever. New censors will need to be added on all of our road networks to accommodate this technology. The rollout of this tech has been problematic. Tesla's electric vehicles have been the subject matter for hundreds of YouTube videos for their auto-pilot mode shenanigans. In the end, these vehicles will never fully adapt to our transportation systems as there is one major component that still exists on our roads: humans. With what we now know about the Federal government's inclination to rely on safety as an excuse for further regulations, it would not be presumptuous to state that bans on all human-controlled vehicles could be a reality in the near future. How will the "internet of things" work effectively with the massive amount of data traffic that will be required?

The transportation network built within the Agenda 2030 smart cities will have a new ally in the war on global contagions with the aftermath of COVID-19. The grid will now enable authoritarian lockdowns, as envisioned in the Rockefeller Foundation's LOCKSTEP scenario, and unprecedented tracking of individuals and collection of their data. In June of 2019, Microsoft applied for a patent that will send users' health data from an embedded device that will be integrated into the cryptocurrency network for a "rewards-based system," based on user data from interactions with advertisements and individual exercise.[71]

ABSTRACT: Human body activity associated with a task provided to a user may be used in a mining process of a cryptocurrency system. A server may provide a task to a device of a user which is communicatively coupled to the server. A sensor communicatively coupled to or comprised in the device of the user may sense body activity of the user. Body activity data may be generated based on the sensed body activity of the user. The cryptocurrency system communicatively coupled to the device of the user may verify if the body activity data satisfies one or more conditions set by the

---

[70] Tim Gruver, "States Consider Taxing Drivers by the Mile despite Privacy Concerns," POLITICO (POLITICO, June 9, 2017), https://www.politico.com/story/2017/06/08/states-consider-taxing-drivers-by-the-mile-despite-privacy-concerns-239336)

[71] Abramson, Dustin, Fu, Derrick and Johnson, Joseph Edwin, JR. 1986. CRYPTOCURRENCY SYSTEM USING BODY ACTIVITY DATA. International Application Number PCT/US2019/038084, filed June 20, 2019.

cryptocurrency system, and award cryptocurrency to the user whose body activity data is verified.[72]

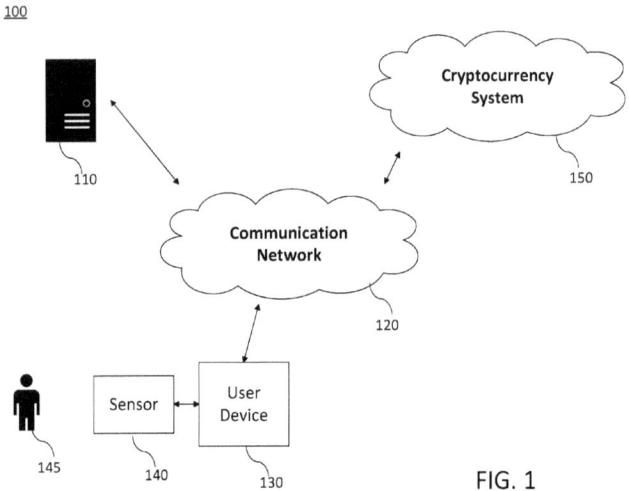

Figure (C) Patent for RFID Chip-Crypto Integration.

The internet of things will enable a system where people's actions, physical movement, and economic activity will be controlled under a global network.

The rollout of 5G cellular internet technology is being advertised as the main component necessary for America to push forward into the future with progressive "smart" cities with the specific intention of rolling out these new technologies. 5G technology requires new radio towers to be installed at every corner and throughout large buildings to work effectively as it only covers short distances. The entire network will make the concept of the "internet of things" possible, which will enable an all-encompassing control grid for applications like tracking GPS bracelets for COVID-19 victims or embedded microchips in the

[72] Abramson et al., "CRYPTOCURRENCY SYSTEM USING BODY ACTIVITY DATA," patentscope.wipo.int, March 26, 2020, https://patentscope.wipo.int/search/en/detail.jsf?docId=WO2020060606&tab=PCTBIBLIO))

wrist that contain all necessary health record data.[73] [74] According to estimates, "10 to 20 billion connections will be part of the internet of things."[75] If people think this type of infrastructure will only be used as a utility for convenience, they are dead wrong.

Although it is being sold to the public as something that will make life more safe and convenient, there will undoubtedly be harmful consequences from this type of infrastructure. In 2015, over 200 doctors and scientists signed on to a letter warning the public of the possible consequences of 5G technology:

> …With the ever more extensive use of wireless technologies, nobody can avoid to be exposed [to RF-EMF radiation] … Effects include increased cancer risk, cellular stress, increase in harmful free radicals, genetic damages, structural and functional changes of the reproductive system, learning and memory deficits, neurological disorders, and negative impacts on general well-being in humans. Damage goes well beyond the human race, as there is growing evidence of harmful effects to both plants and animals.[76]

More research must be done before we construct the 5G network nationwide. Unfortunately, the program is moving forward full-steam ahead. Both the Democratic and Republican parties support 5G technology; President Trump signed the Secure and Trusted Communications Networks Act on March 12, 2020, which specifically labels 5G as the technology of the future.[77]

Why is this relevant to Agenda 2030? All of the above-mentioned tracking devices will be used to restrain mobility and functionality for the average citizen under the auspice of maintaining sustainable development. Since Agenda 2030 aims

[73] Kala Kachmar and Darcy Costello, "Louisville Is Forcing Unwilling Coronavirus Patients to Self-Isolate. Is It Right?," Journal (Louisville Courier Journal, April 3, 2020), https://www.courier-journal.com/story/news/2020/03/31/louisville-circuit-court-ankle-bracelets-noncompliant-coronavirus-patients/5094594002/)

[74] Haley Weiss, "Why You're Probably Getting a Microchip Implant Someday," The Atlantic (Atlantic Media Company, September 21, 2018), https://www.theatlantic.com/technology/archive/2018/09/how-i-learned-to-stop-worrying-and-love-the-microchip/570946/)

[75] "The Appeal," 5G Appeal, March 4, 2019, http://www.5gappeal.eu/scientists-and-doctors-warn-of-potential-serious-health-effects-of-5g/)

[76] Ibid.

[77] "President Donald J. Trump Is Committed To Safeguarding America's Vital Communications Networks And Securing 5G Technology," The White House (The United States Government, March 12, 2020), https://www.whitehouse.gov/briefings-statements/president-donald-j-trump-committed-safeguarding-americas-vital-communications-networks-securing-5g-technology/)

to curb carbon emissions, the scope of control is nearly unlimited. Agenda 2030 and the technology that enables it is not simply limited to the control of carbon emissions. Its main objective is to gain full control over people's daily lives by instilling fear into the public: fear of emitting too much pollution, and fear of contracting deadly viruses "due to overpopulation." Without a doubt, new computer technology has served as the ultimate utility for implementing Agenda 2030. These systems are being dubbed as "smart cities" and represent the ultimate technical culmination of the goals of Agenda 2030 and similar sustainable development programs. When this reality is held in mind with the fact that land ownership is becoming more restricted, the threat Agenda 2030 poses to individual liberty becomes apparent.

To maintain this type of regulatory system, it must remain popular among the local populace. The rise of the internet has allowed for easy delivery of pro-Agenda 2030 propaganda. For the propaganda to remain effective, the thoughts and ideas of citizens must be examined and tracked. Without a doubt, social media serves as the perfect utility for maintaining social control. In order to maintain the new technocratic order, any dissent must be restricted and eventually ignored. This is why Twitter, Facebook, Google, and even Amazon are focusing on restricting what they deem as "hate speech," which is just an excuse to ignore the 1st Amendment. The new technocracy will not accept any form of dissent. Facebook's new "false news" censorship campaign creates an army of "fact-checkers" who have been specifically hired to disqualify information they deem invalid. Many of these online snitches work for large news corporations like CNN.[78] This structure is a soft-kill strategy; the end game is a system based on China's "social credit score" system, where citizens are assigned an individual score for how well they follow the laws and recommendations from their government.

When the power of social media networks is combined with the NSA's controversial surveillance grid under its PRISM program, the activity-based intelligence structure becomes insurmountable. PRISM monitors all citizens' social media, internet activity, and telephone calls, among other things. When former

[78] Todd Starnes, "Facebook Using Company Run by Former CNN Staffer to Target Conservatives," Todd Starnes (Todd Starnes, February 24, 2020), https://www.toddstarnes.com/values/facebook-using-company-run-by-former-cnn-staffer-to-target-conservatives/)

CIA director David Petraeus claimed that America's spy agencies could "spy on you through your dishwasher," he was not joking:

> Items of interest will be located, identified, monitored, and remotely controlled through technologies such as radio-frequency identification, sensor networks, tiny embedded servers, and energy harvesters – all connected to the next-generation internet using abundant, low-cost, and high-power computing," Petraeus said, "the latter now going to cloud computing, in many areas greater and greater supercomputing, and, ultimately, heading to quantum computing.[79]

These events may seem separate; however, with further examination, it is clear that these programs all have one thing in common: they all work with each other to meet the same end. Agenda 2030 represents the ultimate control grid where all human activity is regulated, controlled, or sometimes banned altogether. It represents the implementation of a new technocratic social order.

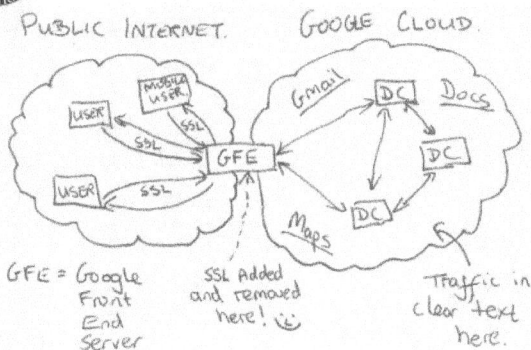

[79] Spencer Ackerman, "CIA Chief: We'll Spy on You Through Your Dishwasher," Wired (Conde Nast, June 3, 2017), https://www.wired.com/2012/03/petraeus-tv-remote/)

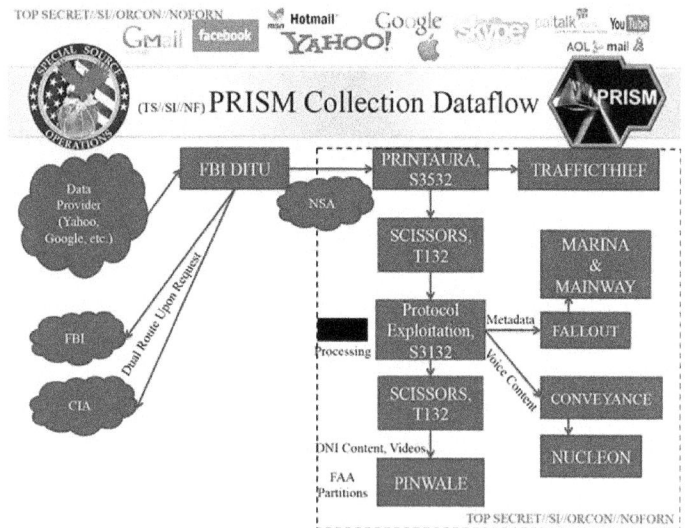

Figure (D) Prism Data Collection Slides, Washington Post.[80]

The concept of environmentalism and sustainable devel-

[80] Prism Collection Documents. The Washington Post, accessed September 20, 2020, https://www.washingtonpost.com/wp-srv/special/politics/prism-collection-documents/)

opment has evolved into an excuse for control freaks and power brokers to take control of local governments, state governments, and the Federal government in order to implement a communist plan with Agenda 2030. The organizations that support this agenda have subverted the US Constitution and State constitutions. The Tenth Amendment of the Constitution states: "The powers not delegated to the United States by the Constitution, nor prohibited by it to the states, are reserved to the States respectively, or to the people."[81] This Amendment is relevant because many policies supporting sustainable development have been enacted via executive order instead of through legislation passed by Congress. These executive orders and the legislation passed by Congress that supports Agenda 2030 directly conflicts with the powers expressly delegated to the US government. Much of this abuse comes from the overly used "commerce clause" in the US Constitution, which states that Congress has the power "to regulate Commerce with foreign Nations, and among the several States, and with the Indian Tribes."[82] Most social issues are intertwined with economic ones, which provides the legal pretext necessary to expand governmental power under this provision. For this reason, it has arguably become the most abused section within the Constitution, and the sustainable development movement has relied heavily on it.

Agenda 2030 continually references the fact that local participation and support is essential to its success. However, the representatives of these fifty states were not present at this UN conference in 1992. Just as the UN does not have the right to dictate affairs in a sovereign country, the Federal Government does not have the right to subjugate states to unwarranted and unconstitutional regulation that is not specifically delegated to them. Simultaneously, with the help of ICLEI, local governments should not be able to subvert State and Federal laws. The Constitution has something called the "supremacy clause," which organizes power based on the fact that the Constitution is the supreme law of the land. In essence, ICLEI found a loophole within America's political system to enact policy change at the local level, effectively bypassing legislation at the national level,

---

[81] US Constitution, Amend. X.

[82] US Constitution, art. I, sec. 8, cl. 3.

which can often be a slow and arduous process.

Agenda 2030 has no deference for the concept of private property. By restricting land use to the point where land ownership becomes impossible, the concept of private property is ultimately destroyed. The Fourteenth Amendment states: "… no state shall deprive any person of life, liberty, or property, without due process of law."[83] James Madison continues: "as a man is said to have a right to his property, he may be equally said to have a property in his rights."[84]Surely, the Bundy family sees the value in these proclamations. Additionally, the Constitution never mentions the power to force citizens to purchase specific products over another. Regardless of whether an item is more energy-efficient than its counterparts, the consumer should have the right to choose what works better for their current situation. It is evident that Agenda 2030 has completely ignored the United States Constitution and the rule of law.

If Agenda 2030 were to be put in action, the overall cost to all nations would exceed hundreds of billions of dollars. Most would contend that this number is large and would effectively cripple any nation's economy during times of economic crises. However, Agenda 2030 feels otherwise: "The cost of inaction could outweigh the financial costs of implementing Agenda 2030. Inaction will narrow the choices of future generations."[85] This may be effective during economic expansions, but this cannot be considered feasible when countries cannot afford to commit financial resources when they are bankrupt. Furthermore, because Agenda 2030 dictates how countries should trade their commodities and how to run domestic economic policies, it would have to garner full support from all nations. Not only does this feat seem impossible, but it would effectively have to remove sovereign control from all nations as well. If one country decides not to contribute to the program, it can be assumed that all other countries would "gang up" on this lone wolf. In essence, not only does Agenda 2030 aim to curb carbon footprints, but

---

83 US Constitution, Amend. XIV.

84 "Protecting Private Property Rights from Regulatory Takings," Cato Institute, December 15, 2012, https://www.cato.org/publications/congressional-testimony/protecting-private-property-rights-regulatory-takings)

85 "Agenda 21" (United Nations, 1992), https://sustainabledevelopment.un.org/content/documents/Agenda21.pdf, Ch.33)

it also aims to set illegitimate price controls on all countries involved. Numerous studies report that AOC's "Green New Deal" will cost approximately $2.5 trillion per year. With these costs considered, there is no doubt that the ultimate goal is to bankrupt the world's economy to implement a new communist economic and social order with Agenda 2030.

There is no doubt that humans have some sort of impact on their natural environment. However, it is vital to validate this argument with the Scientific Method. The recent "Climategate" scandal proves that scientists were altering data schemes to successfully argue that climate change is human-caused.[86] They falsified their data. For people who are supposedly attempting to save the world, what is the need for lying? It is undeniable that egocentric politicians have helped push the theory that climate change is solely driven by human activity. Agenda 2030 recommends "governments and private-sector organizations should promote more positive attitudes towards sustainable consumption through education, public awareness programmes and other means…."[87] Is it not true that the purpose of education is to examine all possible outcomes and solutions? What happened to the concept of critical thinking? When education systems abstain only to promote one side of the story, they are not educating; they are only serving up a fresh plate of propaganda. For society to thoroughly understand the causes of climate change, we must examine every possible outcome. This point is especially valid if we are about to create a new way of life that is entirely based on the theory that mankind is ultimately a detriment to the world, rather than a welcomed inhabitant that is included within the global biosphere.

Overall, the issues surrounding sustainable development and the environmentalist movement are very involved with a rich history. Most of the evidence that they provide is very credible and cannot be ignored. No one wants to breathe dirty air or drink poisoned water from a dirty well. However, the overall solution for these calamities will either promote freedom or destroy it.

[86] Fox News, "Climategate 2.0? More Emails Leaked From Climate Researchers," Fox News (FOX News Network, December 18, 2014), https://www.foxnews.com/science/climategate-2-0-more-emails-leaked-from-climate-researchers)

[87] "Agenda 21" (United Nations, 1992), https://sustainabledevelopment.un.org/content/documents/Agenda21.pdf, Ch.4)

115

The United States government has always negotiated with other countries on the premise of volunteerism. We have always promoted democracy because we felt it would always support the concept of individual liberty and freedom. Many countries caught on to this new trend; many recognized it as the best form of government. The concepts that surround sustainable development should be implemented voluntarily and only through the facilities of the free market or the voting booth. In doing so, any new theory must be validated through the scientific method and then enforced with the rule of law with the people's full support. Regardless of the solutions and the subsequent devices for them, the ethical integrity of Agenda 2030 has been compromised. The scientific conclusions it is based on has been proven to be fraudulent. It seeks to destroy the concept of private property and consumer choice. It seeks to promote legislation that reflects the ideologies of Karl Marx instead of the ideals promoted by a free-market society. In the end, Agenda 2030 is a communist plot hidden behind the morally advantageous "green" movement. The world's elite have come together in a communist conspiracy to control the planet through an all-powerful technocracy where citizens are treated like peasants in a new-age feudalist society. If America and other countries refuse to observe the actual consequences of Agenda 2030, our entire way of life will cease to exist.

VI

Californication and the Colorado Method

If you talk to any native Coloradan, they will have no problem acknowledging that Colorado has changed for the worse. On either side of the political spectrum, most Coloradans would readily admit that the recent population influx has put a strain on the state's resources and way of life. As one native says, "it seems like you are waiting in a queue line at an amusement park, just to go on a hike in the front range!" As far as politics go, many feel it is the direct source of cultural change. For conservative and libertarian Coloradans they feel that Colorado has fallen off of a socialist cliff. They are right. Colorado is no longer a red state; those days passed a long time ago. Colorado is no longer a purple state either; that change was solidified with the outcome of the 2018 midterm elections. Colorado is now solidly blue. This change is not by accident, billionaires and socialist politicians have had Colorado in their sights for many years, and they can now claim victory.

Before Colorado's takeover, another western state has lost its free spirit to Marxist politicians. Many people have forgotten that California once elected Ronald Reagan as Governor in 1967 and later as President in 1981. It is hard to imagine this with the current policies coming out of the state today. What exactly happened to California's electorate? Many scholars have contended that legal and illegal immigration has wholly altered the state's political make-up. Without a doubt, California leads the nation for the number of illegal immigrants as a percentage of the population. Between 1960 and 1995, the number of immigrants living in the state increased from 1.3 million to eight million and tripled as a percentage of the state's population, from 8.2 percent to 24.1 percent. California also had a lower rate of naturalization at 29 percent.[1] Conservative pundit Wayne Allyn Root of the Las Vegas Review puts it best:

> I have the No. 1 lie in America for you: Diversity makes us stronger, and immigration makes us more prosperous...Cal-

[1] Steven A. Camarota, "The Impact of Immigration on California," CIS.org (Center for Immigration Studies, July 1, 1998), https://cis.org/Report/Impact-Immigration-California)

117

ifornia leads the nation in debt. Total state and local debt is almost $1.5 trillion. Combining state debt with California's share of federal debt produces a debt-to-GDP ratio of 153 percent — higher than the PIGS of the EU (Portugal, Italy, Greece, and Spain), which are all facing economic collapse and ruin…The income taxes, business taxes, sales taxes and gas taxes are all the highest in the nation. Why do you think that is? To pay [for] the enormous costs of illegal immigration.[2]

It is undeniable that there is a strong argument to be made on the correlation between the rising illegal immigration population and the rise in welfare expenditures and the overall cost of living.

In reality, migrants are simply a tool for the Marxist elite to change the electorate in their favor. From the 1960s onward, California was already at the forefront of progressive policy, even before its elections had swung steadfastly for the Democrats. The UN Agenda 2030 communist program is heavily influenced by the same policies that endorsed eugenics in America's early 20th century. Whether it is using people to manipulate demographics for elections or recommending lower population levels, progressive policies have always been based on population control. California has always led the way for the rest of the country regarding eugenics policies. In 1909 after forced sterilization laws were passed for the "mentally defective," California had more sterilizations than any other state in the country. Shockingly, forced sterilizations continued in the state up until 1963.[3] At the height of the eugenics movement in the United States and before World War II, the German Reich had praised the United States' efforts to control its population. Hitler once told Otto Wagner, head of the Nazi Party's Economic Policy Office (1931-1933), "I have studied with great interest the laws of several American states concerning prevention of reproduction by people whose progeny would, in all probability, be of

---

[2] Wayne Allyn Root, "COMMENTARY: Illegal Immigrants Have Turned California into the American Nightmare," Review Journal (Las Vegas Review-Journal, November 9, 2018), https://www.reviewjournal.com/opinion/opinion-columns/wayne-allyn-root/commentary-illegal-immigrants-have-turned-california-into-the-american-nightmare/)

[3] Lutz Kaelber, "California Eugenics," Eugenics: Compulsory Sterilization in 50 American States (University of Vermont, March 4, 2009), https://www.uvm.edu/~lkaelber/eugenics/CA/CA.html)

no value or be injurious to the racial stock...."[4] Charles Goethe, president of the Eugenics Research Association in California, returned the compliment to Hitler:

> The Reich today has her social inadequacies more thoroughly listed than any other nation... [T]o a land whose population approaches the saturation point, elimination by sterilization of those unfit means room for higher power. It is well known...that Germany's leaders in the sterilization movement depended mostly upon the material collected by the California data foundation upon which to rear their present remarkable structure...[5] [6]

It is undeniable that California is ground-zero for the modern eugenics movement and Marxist ideology in America.

The organizations that helped create California's eugenics program are the same institutions that helped found the United Nations, namely the Rockefeller Foundation. These groups have all worked together to push their communist, neo-fascist agenda forward in America. For the United States, California is leading the way for the globalists. For the last fifty years, the systemic spread of socialism has been confined to the borders of California and other states that are controlled by the globalists, like New York. The communists at the United Nations have been stymied in their attempts to take their new political and economic structure nationwide and eventually worldwide. However, California's economic and cultural collapse has sent its residents fleeing to other states, inexorably changing the US electorate. This situation has proven to be an excellent opportunity for those looking to expand California's vision for America.

On the one hand, there is a wave of ex-Californians migrating to other states who have notably maintained their socialist voting behavior. On the other, you have a small group of socialist California millionaires and billionaires and NGOs attempting to influence other states' elections. The combina-

[4] Stefan Kuhl, *Nazi Connection Eugenics, American Racism, and German National Socialism* (Cary: Oxford University Press, USA, 2014), p.37-39)

[5] Randall Hansen and Desmond S King, *Sterilized by the State: Eugenics, Race, and the Population Scare in Twentieth-Century North America* (Cambridge: Cambridge University Press, 2013), p.154)

[6] Katherine Stolerman, "The American Eugenics Movement: A Study of the Dispersal and Application of Racial Ideologies" (Aisthesis, November 2, 2017), https://pubs.lib.umn.edu/index.php/aisthesis/article/view/49, p.18)

tion serves as the ultimate catalyst to permanently change other states' political environment to their standards. In backdoor rooms across the country, meetings were held to discuss the well-organized plan to take down America. For this to occur, a process must be developed. This political recipe must be a process that can be repeated no matter the local political environment. What happened to California must be exported to every state in America.

Colorado is the newly chosen state for progressive policy. Its political transformation serves as the ultimate blueprint to adopt the communist Agenda 2030 program nationwide. California's political kingpins are now looking to expand their influence by consolidating their efforts towards flipping other states one by one. By allying itself with California's politics, Colorado has set course on a path towards inevitable economic and cultural destruction. Once a state that boasted about its level of independent voting, balanced politics, and low cost of living, Colorado now serves as conquered territory for billionaire socialists, where crime and the cost of living have skyrocketed. The state ultimately represents the true political bellwether for America. It is necessary to examine why Colorado was chosen by progressives and the financial elite to enact their agenda and how other states can avoid similar transformations in the future. We will examine Colorado's cultural and political history to illustrate its political takeover by the Democratic party. The analysis will show that the proponents of the United Nations' Marxist Agenda 2030 have infiltrated Colorado to enact their plans nationwide. Instead of focusing their resources on national elections, they have decided to transform the nation by changing one state at a time, like cancer attacks one cell in the human body at a time.

How did Colorado's Marxist political revolution occur? Colorado's transformation is a consequence of both planned and unplanned circumstances. The agenda to transform Colorado has been well documented by the financial dealings of progressive millionaires and billionaires and nongovernmental organizations. This massive influx of outside funding has directly led to success for Colorado Democrats in the state legislature. The individuals and organizations that support this plan have focused their efforts on amplifying the Demographic wave that Colorado is experiencing to tilt the electorate in their favor. Simultaneously, the Marxists that support Agenda 2030 have ensured that their values will be reinforced by controlling local school districts and their curriculums. This could not have occurred without a blatant stand-down from supposed liberty-minded patriots in Colorado. Residents of Nevada, Idaho, Montana, Texas, and Virginia should pay close attention to these tactics as these states are also experiencing an influx of change, whether it be by an increase in new residents with differing ideological backgrounds or an increase in outside funding and manipulation from NGOs and billionaire political activists.

A Seismic Demographic Shift

Colorado's transformation did not come overnight. The infamous Colorado license plate bumper stickers that say "NO VACANCY" or "NATIVE" have been around for over thirty years. Colorado natives have had no problem vocalizing their disdain for recent population influxes into the state. Ultimately, increased population and the demographics of those who are moving to Colorado represent some of the main contributing factors to Colorado's political and cultural transformation. The secret has been out for some time: Colorado has beautiful weather, an impressive landscape, and an adventurous spirit. Colorado has attracted people from all over the nation and all over the world. Since 1970, Colorado has gained just over 3.5 million residents.[7] The Denver Post was proud to announce in 2018 that Colorado was the 7th fastest-growing state in America.[8] The demographics of those who are moving here are also something that cannot necessarily be predicted. It can only be measured and analyzed once the migration has occurred. Politically and culturally speaking, Colorado is attracting residents from states who tend to lean far left, such as California, Illinois, New York, and New Mexico.[9] With Colorado trending to the left in recent years, policies have

[7] "Colorado Population 1900-2019," MacroTrends, accessed March 18, 2020, https://www.macrotrends.net states/colorado/population)

[8] Sam Tabachnik, "With 80,000 New Residents, Colorado Is the Seventh-Fastest Growing State in the US," The Denver Post (The Denver Post, December 24, 2018), https://www.denverpost.com/2018/12/24/colorado-population-growth/)

[9] Amy Zimmer, "Who's Moving Into and Out of Colorado?," Colorado Virtual Library, December 17, 2018, https://www.coloradovirtuallibrary.org/resource-sharing/state-pubs-blog/whos-moving-into-and-out-of-colorado/)

also attracted leftist elements from those leaving states dominated by conservatives. The result is a state that votes completely blue. These circumstances are often unavoidable. If other states have issues with their economies, or if there is a sudden change in culture, it is not unexpected to see their residents flee to more desirable states. Historically, Colorado had maintained a healthy level of Independents, Democrats, and Republicans with almost an even three-way split. Yet, in recent years the voter registration data shows that Colorado's independent voter base has increased to 40 percent. Democrats hold a 29 to 28 percent lead over Republicans in Colorado, and currently hold majorities in the statehouse, senate, and governorship.[10] This begs the question of whether or not Independents in Colorado tend to vote more for Democrats. According to the Colorado Secretary of State 2018 election primary results, Colorado's unaffiliated voters selected Democrat ballots over Republicans 2 to 1.[11] Although these unaffiliated voters claim to have no allegiance, the data clearly shows otherwise.

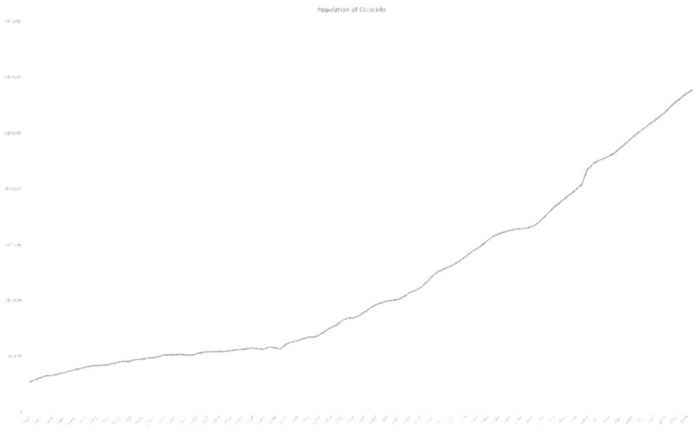

Figure (A) Population of Colorado, US Census Bureau, Accessed August, 2020.

[10] John Frank, "Colorado Hits a New Milestone with Unaffiliated Voters and Busts the Myth about Its Even Partisan Split," The Colorado Sun (The Colorado Sun, December 26, 2019), https://coloradosun.com/2019/12/26/colorado-voter-registration-unaffiliated-voters-2020-election/)

[11] "2018 Ballots Received "(Colorado Secretary of State, June 27, 2018), https://www.sos.state.co.us/pubs/newsRoom/pressReleases/2018/20180627BallotsReceivedByAgePartyGender.pdf)

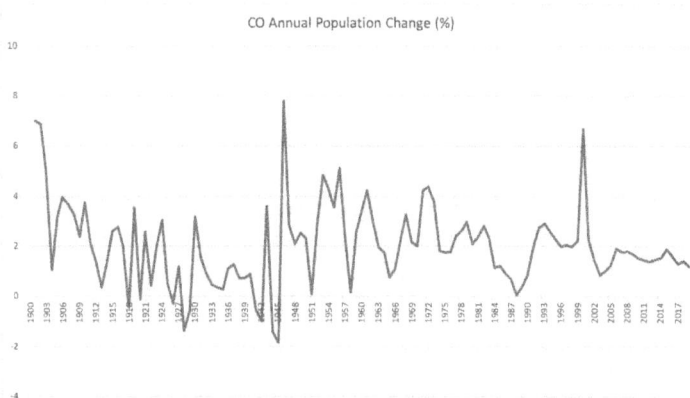

CO Annual Population Change (%)

Figure (B) Colorado Annual Population Change, BLS, Accessed August, 2020.

      Secondly, Colorado has experienced a hefty rise in illegal and legal immigration from third-world countries in the last thirty years, contributing to a new demographic wave. Colorado Democrats have instituted policy changes that are attractive to these new residents, such as obtaining a driver's license, mail-in voting, and access to welfare. This demographic shift has enabled the Democratic party to change elections in their favor. Driver's license offices offer voter registration where fake social security numbers can be used[12], and mail-in voting is highly susceptible to fraud. Colorado has already investigated multiple instances of voter fraud related to loopholes within the absentee voting process.[13] Those that immigrate here legally from these countries often rely on welfare and other forms of government assistance, as compared to native citizens. The Center for Immigration Studies reported in 2018 that 63 percent of non-citizen households access welfare programs.[14] It is only logical to assume that those who are addicted to welfare programs will likely

[12] Joel Rose, "The Latest Immigration Crackdown May Be Fake Social Security Numbers," NPR (NPR, March 29, 2019), https://www.npr.org/2019/03/29/707931619/social-security-administration-plans-to-revive-no-match-letters)

[13] Jesse Paul, "10 People in Colorado May Have Cast Two Ballots in 2016 Election, While 38 Might Have Also Voted in Another State, Study Says," The Denver Post (The Denver Post, September 15, 2017), https://www.denverpost.com/2017/09/15/colorado-2016-improper-voting-study/)

[14] Steven A. Camarota and Karen Zeigler, "63% Of Non-Citizen Households Access Welfare Programs," CIS.org (Center for Immigration Studies, November 20, 2018), https://cis.org/Report/63-NonCitizen-Households-Access-Welfare-Programs)

vote for politicians who promise to keep the money flowing. This is arguably the most important facet of the American Marxist strategy to transform local politics. Democrats are well aware of the loopholes hidden within our nation's election system, and population manipulation is one of them.

Thirdly, Colorado has seen plenty of investment from the Federal government since its founding. Colorado is home to the US Air Force, Buckley Air Force Base, Petersen Air Force Base, Buckley Air Force Base, Cheyenne Mountain/NORAD, The Federal Center, Lockheed Martin, Raytheon, and others. Colorado is among the top ten states with the most Federal government employees next to Washington, D.C.[15] Consequently, the demographic shift in Colorado is both a natural phenomenon and a planned one. There is massive investment in the state from the federal government and the companies that support it. It should be no surprise to anyone that a state with a high composition of government workers is likely to lean towards policy-making which supporters more government, not less. The democrats have been able to curb these shifts in their favor, and it has catalyzed the Marxist makeover of the state.

Education

Before these massive population influxes, Colorado democrats had obtained control of Colorado's education system and other services, which would undoubtedly help them secure more political power in the future. Ultimately, it was a "soft-kill" strategy, whereby Democrats would control things like the school districts, local municipalities, recreation, and transportation districts. It is undeniable that their control over Colorado's education system has had the most substantial impact, which has led to a new generation of progressives, ready to vote for more government intervention across the board. Speaking to one Colorado native, he complained of "the overall lack of education on things like the Constitution, property rights, and the importance of the 2nd amendment. Much of the social studies classes focused on a socialist, outcomes-based economy. The science

---

[15] Darla Cameron, Dan Keating, and Armand Emamdjomeh, "Analysis | Where Do Federal Workers-Live?," The Washington Post (WP Company, August 30, 2018), https://www.washingtonpost.com/graphics/2018/politics/federal-workers/)

classes were mainly focused on the threat of mankind to the environment. In other words, everything was about the importance of government intervention."[16] This Colorado Republican's complaints directly relate to the policies endorsed by the "Common Core" education system. Common Core regularly defers to "outcomes-based learning," which relies heavily on testing for both students and teachers alike. Charlotte Iserbyt, a former senior policy adviser for the Department of Education under Ronald Reagan and author of *The Deliberate Dumbing Down of America*, has consistently decried new education standards as a communist conspiracy to transform America's education system into Marxist/Trotskyite indoctrination centers:

> The goal since the 1900s is to create a socialist global system...to create the new Soviet man...a world full of worker bees...I'm talking about the school to work agenda [which is] definitely a communist agenda, funded by the Carnegie Foundation...I call 'Common Core' 'Communist Core,' because that's exactly what it is.[17]

There was one bout of resistance with the election of three conservative school board members in Jefferson County. However, they were quickly recalled for pulling back on some of the Marxist curriculum standards and endorsing a voucher program for charter schools, which is also attached to this communist agenda, according to Iserbyt.[18]

After the Columbine Massacre at Columbine High School in April of 1999, Colorado was thrown into the national spotlight for gun control policies, bullying, and overall school safety. The precautionary principle that was already prominent in Colorado's schools became the ultimate tool for the situation at hand. The infamous "zero tolerance" policy for bullying and fighting changed school policies statewide forever. Topics like bullying and personal relationships are no longer treated as a future discussion between parent and child, where self-reliance was taught. Instead, it demanded government intervention where

---

[16] Anonymous 2012 Colorado Congressional Republican Delegate. Interview by H. Nicholas Scott. Phone Interview. Denver, CO. January 26th, 2020.

[17] Charlotte Iserbyt, "Charlotte Iserbyt - Common Core - Save Long Island Forum 1/18/14," YouTube (We Are Change CT, January 25, 2014), https://www.youtube.com/watch?v=OA5zStXdGlo)

[18] Ibid.

everyone involved should be punished, regardless of the situation. If a teenage boy defends oneself from a group of bullies, he or she is charged with a crime for fighting back. What should be respected as a natural response in a fight or flight situation is now a crime. The event galvanized the "2ⁿᵈ-wave feminism" generation that blamed "toxic masculinity" for the world's problems. In the end, common sense approaches were disregarded entirely. Christina Hoff Sommers astutely observes in her book *The War Against Boys: How Misguided Feminism is Harming Our Young Men* that "…we are turning against boys and forgetting a simple truth: that the energy, competitiveness, and corporal daring of normal, decent males is responsible for much of what is right in the world…boys need love and understanding, they do not need to be pathologized."[19] Colorado's political and cultural climate now represents the ultimate rallying cry for implementing progressive educational policies in schools nationwide.

After the Aurora theater shooting, the calls for gun control in a state that had not yet healed its wounds from Columbine once again dominated the political discussion across the country. This is another crisis that politicians and Government bureaucrats did not "let go to waste." In many ways, Colorado's political climate presented the perfect petri dish for progressives through no fault of its own.

Outside Influence and Jared Polis

To obtain full control of Colorado, the Democratic Party had to find a way to attract independent voters and overwhelm the state with new Democrats. Democrat donors poured massive funding into the state. The story of Colorado's transformation is highlighted in Adam Schrager and Rob Witwer's book, *The Blueprint: How Democrats Won Colorado.* Their book focuses on the Democrats' overall strategy to flip Colorado from a red/purple state to solid blue. Their book's most important revelation is their research into the highly influential "Gang of Four," a group of millionaires and billionaires hell-bent on stripping Colorado Republicans of their power. Jared Polis, Pat Stryker, Tim Gill, and Rutt Bridges are undeniably the main conspirators

---

[19] Christina Hoff. Sommers, *The War against Boys: How Misguided Feminism Is Harming Our Young Men* (New York, NY: Simon & Schuster, 2001), p.14)

behind the Democrats' takeover of Colorado. Although Colorado's political transition has occurred slowly over time, these four billionaire-turned-activists presided over a campaign that took the Democrats over the top in terms of political domination. How did they do it?

The story of these four power brokers is one of complete irony and hypocrisy. It is considerably ironic that Colorado's transition from a Republican-led state to a Democratic one came from the leadership of four billionaires in a hidden back room instead of a grassroots uprising from the party who claims to abhor money's influence in politics. Most would find it completely hypocritical that four billionaires who clamored for campaign finance reform in public also worked to find every loophole in the rule book to directly fund their Democratic State House and Senate campaigns in Colorado. For a historian or political scientist, these observations are not surprising. Corruption and politics fit together like O.J. Simpson's hand fit with his infamous glove. According to current Colorado Governor Jared Polis, "[they] ran it like a business."[20] What specifically did the Gang of Four do to ensure their funding would have an immediate impact in Colorado politics?

After campaign finance reform in the early 2000s, it became illegal for political parties and their candidates to work directly with non-profit organizations. This temporarily halted funding to political campaigns. However, "527" organizations (named after the specific section of the federal tax law that they are listed for) allow for private citizens to donate to them on an almost unlimited basis, which then "indirectly" lobby for specific candidates and parties. The tax law is a sad, pathetic attempt by the Federal Government to limit corruption in politics. All they did was create a new type of political organization to give donors like the "Gang of Four" unlimited access to political resources. These groups were allowed to work with each other with no limitations whatsoever, and the Gang of Four exploited this loophole. According to Schrager and Witwer, they used four principal 527 organizations to enact their agenda: Alliance for Colorado's Families, Forward Colorado, Coalition for a Better Colorado

---

[20] "How the Dems Won Colorado," The Denver Post (The Denver Post, April 8, 2010), https://www.denverpost.com/2010/04/08/how-the-dems-won-colorado/)

and Alliance for a Better Colorado.[21] All of these organizations worked vigorously to flip the Colorado State House and Senate for the Democrats. They already knew they could consistently hold onto the governorship, as history as shown. Democrat governors like Hickenlooper did a great job at transforming the judiciary while Polis' crew was focused on taking over the rest of the government. Of the $3.6 Million raised by Democrat 527 organizations, almost $2.5 million was raised by the "Gang of Four" alone. On the other side of the aisle, the Republican 527s raised just under $850,000.[22] So much for the idea that the Republican Party is the "party of the rich."

A group of likely former Jared Polis supporters, who are clamoring for more government intervention in the market.

The "Gang of Four" were not alone in their efforts. California billionaire Tom Steyer's environmental organization NextGen Climate Action put up $50,000,000 in Colorado's 2014 midterm election alone[23], and in 2016 he donated approximately

21 Ibid.

22 "How the Dems Won Colorado," The Denver Post (The Denver Post, April 8, 2010), https://www.denverpost.com/2010/04/08/how-the-dems-won-colorado/)

23 Lynn Bartels, "Climate Change Guru Tom Steyer Donates Big Bucks to Help Mark Udall," The Denver Post (The Denver Post, April 27, 2016), https://www.denverpost.com/2014/05/22/climate-change-guru-tom-steyer-donates-big-bucks-to-help-mark-udall/)

$91,000,000 to democrats nationwide.[24] Steyer's main objective is to push the sustainable development agenda forward. He has made strong efforts to restrict the oil and gas industry, especially in northern Colorado.

New York billionaire Michael Bloomberg donated $50 million to his gun control group Everytown for Gun Safety in 2014, which targeted elections in fifteen states, including Colorado.[25] In 2019, he laid out his gun control agenda in Aurora, Colorado for the political optics. His plan calls for a ban on "assault" weapons and high-capacity magazines, permits for gun ownership, a federal extreme risk protection order law, or "red flag law," and raising the minimum age for gun ownership to 21.[26] Without a doubt, it is the most expansive gun control plan among his Democrat colleagues.

George Soros, a progressive billionaire, and admitted Nazi collaborator[27], is also a prominent donor to multiple progressive efforts across Colorado. He has funded elections for Democrats in almost every area of government. Soros has donated money to democrat district attorney candidates, state house and senate candidates, and governor candidates. His political action committee "Immigrant Voters Win," put its sights on Colorado in 2016 to help recruit Latino and immigrant voters to the Democratic party with an initial $15 million budget.[28] In 2016 he backed these Democrat candidates: Rachel Zenzinger (SD-19), Jenise May (SD-25), Daniel Kagan (SD-26), Tony

[24] Tim Hains, "Tom Steyer Says He Became The Biggest Donor In Politics To Advocate For Getting Money Out Of Politics," RealClearPolitics (RealClearPolitics, November 26, 2017), https://www.realclear-politics.com/video/2017/11/26/tom_steyer_says_he_became_the_biggest_donor_in_politics_to_advocate_for_getting_money_out_of_politics.html)

[25] Jeremy W. Peters, "Bloomberg Plans a $50 Million Challenge to the NRA," The New York Times (The New York Times, April 16, 2014), https://www.nytimes.com/2014/04/16/us/bloomberg-plans-a-50-million-challenge-to-the-nra.html)

[26] Blair Miller, "Michael Bloomberg Unveils Anti-Gun Violence Policy at Aurora Town Hall," thedenverchannel (KMGH, December 6, 2019), https://www.thedenverchannel.com/news/local-news/michael-bloomberg-set-to-unveil-anti-gun-violence-policy-at-aurora-town-hall)

[27] Steve Kroft, Interviewer. Dinesh D'Souza YouTube Channel, "George Soros 60 Minutes Interview" (CBS, 1999), https://www.youtube.com/watch?v=X9tKvasRO54&t=7s)

[28] Nicholas Confessore and Julia Preston, "Soros and Other Liberal Donors to Fund Bid to Spur Latino Voters," The New York Times (The New York Times, March 10, 2016), https://www.nytimes.com/2016/03/10/us/politics/george-soros-and-other-liberal-donors-to-fund-bid-to-spur-latino-voters.html)

Exum (HD-17), and Joe Salazar (HD-31).[29] As of 2020, all of these offices are currently held by the Democrats. Soros has continued his election meddling efforts in 2020 by funding Democrat candidates like House Representative Jason Crow and former Governor John Hickenlooper in his run for US Senate.[30] Without a doubt, Colorado's political future has been decided by outside election meddlers and political carpetbaggers.

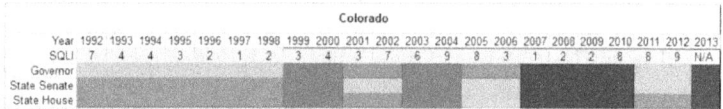

							Colorado															
Year	1992	1993	1994	1995	1996	1997	1998	1999	2000	2001	2002	2003	2004	2005	2006	2007	2008	2009	2010	2011	2012	2013
SQLI	7	4	4	3	2	1	2	3	4	3	7	6	9	8	3	1	2	2	8	8	9	N/A
Governor																						
State Senate																						
State House																						

Figure (C), Colorado Party Majority Historical Chart.

The most recent midterm election in 2018 revealed that a "blue wave" had crashed entirely over all of Colorado. The Democrats swept the State House, the State Senate, and the Governorship. Since their election, they have passed multiple aggressive bills along partisan lines. Many have alleged that their agenda represents the "definition of overreach." **Here is a list of some of the tyrannical laws** passed by the Democrats that will change the state's political landscape forever:

Extreme Risk Protection Order Law HB19-1177 (Red Flag Gun Confiscation Law)

Red-flag laws have become a popular topic of discussion in light of recent mass shootings throughout the United States. In Colorado, the deadly shooting that led to Lone Tree police officer Zachari Parrish's death was the catalyst for this discussion. Simply stated, red-flag laws allow family members and concerned citizens to report someone that owns a gun who may be a danger to themselves or others. The matter goes before a judge after the guns have been confiscated to decide on the matter.

---

[29] Complete Colorado, "Steyer's Got Company: Billionaire George Soros Makes a Play for Colorado's State Legislature," Complete Colorado - Page Two, September 18, 2017, https://pagetwo.completecolorado.com/2016/08/02/steyer-soros-colorado-state-legislature/)

[30] Justin Wingerter, "Soros Family, Private Prison Company Inject Thousands into US Senate Race,"

The Denver Post (The Denver Post, February 7, 2020), https://www.denverpost.com/2020/02/07/fundraising-2020-senate-hickenlooper-gardner/)

There is not a trial; there is no due process. Under the law, **any family member, household member, or law enforcement officer could go before a judge and ask for an extreme risk protection order. A judge could immediately order a person's guns to be taken away if they are deemed a threat. Within 14 days, a formal hearing must occur where the gun owner could request their guns back. The state would provide legal representation. If a judge still deems an individual as a risk, their guns could be taken away for up to 364 days.**[31]

Adoption of California Vehicle Emission Standards

In 2018, the Colorado Air Quality Control Commission enacted rules set by an executive order by former Governor John Hickenlooper, seeking to reduce greenhouse gases by 25 percent by 2025. **Under the rules, new vehicles will be required to average 36 mpg by 2025**, 10 mpg over the existing standard. The rules will add additional costs to larger SUVS and trucks, which are widely used in Colorado's rugged areas.[32]

Ending Colorado's participation in the electoral college

Colorado, along with 13 other states, has entered into a pact to attach their electoral college votes to the national popular vote in response to the election of President Donald J. Trump. Previously, these states had attached their electoral votes to the popular vote for President within their State, not the sum of all other states. The Constitution mentions that individual States do have the power to choose how their electors are chosen and how they vote. However, when these 14 states entered into an agreement with each other to do so, they violated Article I, Section 10 of the Constitution:

> No State shall enter into any Treaty, Alliance, or Confederation; grant Letters of Marque and Reprisal; coin Money; emit Bills of Credit; make any Thing but gold and silver Coin a Tender in Payment of Debts; pass any Bill of Attain-

[31] H.R. Res. 19-1177, Sess. of 2019 (CO. 2019), https://leg.colorado.gov/sites/default/files/2019a_1177_signed.pdf

[32] The Associated Press, "Colorado Adopts California Emissions Standards," Colorado Springs Gazette (Colorado Springs Gazette, February 14, 2020), https://gazette.com/news/colorado-adopts-california-emissions-standards/article_75cf2d4e-e9fc-11e8-9f4b-371bc967a46c.html)

der, ex post facto Law, or Law impairing the Obligation of Contracts, or grant any Title of Nobility.

Through and through, the process for selecting the President was meant to be clear and unambiguous. Democrats in these 14 states have chosen to subvert the original intentions of the Constitution and the will of the American people. Dr. Thomas Krannawitter of *Speakeasy Ideas* states it best:

> *The fundamental purpose of the Electoral College was to help form not merely willful numerical majorities in select-ing Presidents, but reasonable majorities, or, at a mini-mum, moderate majorities, perhaps the closest practical thing to a reasonable majority.[33]*

We live in perilous times. One hundred eighty-nine electoral votes make up the states that have passed this law. They only need 270. It is like holding the election now—for all future elections!

Sanctuary City Status

Without a doubt, the political elites of Boulder and Denver have full control of Colorado politics. Both cities have declared sanctuary city status for illegal immigrants. They have notoriously been in a war of words with President Trump in his attempts to reign in cities that shield offenders from deportation. According to the CBI, Colorado has seen a 25 percent increase in violent crime.[34] Simultaneously, Colorado has risen to 3rd in the country for car insurance premium costs.[35] When the Boulder City Council declared itself a sanctuary city, Mayor Suzanne Jones proclaimed, "we are sending a message of reassurance to the people." [36] Clearly, she is not speaking to the American peo-

---

[33] Dr. Thomas Krannawitter, "Is the Will of the Majority Reasonable?" (Speakeasy Ideas Newsletter, Feb 5, 2019. Accessed March 29, 2020, Email)

[34] Noelle Phillips, "Violent Crime up 25 Percent in Colorado since 2013, Latest CBI Report Shows," The Denver Post (The Denver Post, September 28, 2018), https://www.denverpost.com/2018/09/28/colora-do-crime-data/)

[35] Aldo Svaldi, "Colorado Is No. 3 in the Country for Rising Car Insurance Premiums. Here's Why.," The Denver Post (The Denver Post, February 28, 2018), https://www.denverpost.com/2018/02/27/colora-do-car-insurance-premiums-rise/)

[36] Alex Burness, "Defying Trump, Boulder Declares Itself a Sanctuary City," Daily Camera (Boulder Daily Camera, January 3, 2017), https://www.dailycamera.com/2017/01/03/defying-trump-boulder-declares-it-self-a-sanctuary-city/)

ple or local Coloradans for that matter.

Oppressive, unnecessary oil and gas restrictions

Governor Jared Polis and the Democrats successfully overhauled Colorado's oil and gas rules in 2019 with Senate Bill 19-181[37], with an increased focus on public safety and the environment, rather than increased production. The law gives local governments significant new authority to restrict the location of wells. Colorado voters rejected previous attempts to regulate the industry, but the Democrats moved forward with their new regulations with no regard for the voices of millions of Coloradans. Ironically, the Democratic party always finds ways to ignore the democratic process. Oil and gas analysts have consistently maintained that the law will increase the cost of drilling in Colorado, which would inevitably lead to many companies leaving the state for greener pastures.[38] In reality, this is just another attempt to rezone Colorado as a whole under Agenda 2030 guidelines.

The cowardice of the Colorado GOP

How did the Republican leadership of Colorado respond to these gradual impediments on the liberties of Coloradans? They elected the "good ole' boys" who were fine with going along with the status quo as long as it remained profitable. They were okay with losing the state as long they did not lose their sphere of influence. As comedian George Carlin astutely stated, "NIMBY! Not-In-My-Back-yard!" As long as their inner circle and lifestyle remained intact, forget the other guy. As long as those regulations did not affect their livelihood, it was business-as-usual.

The greatest example of this was the sudden and unexpected spurt of libertarianism Colorado experienced from 2008-2012. Colorado has always been known for its purple, independent roots; however, these years were different. Libertarianism had become popular during these years under the leadership of

[37] SB 19-181, Sess. of 2019 (CO. 2019), https://cogcc.state.co.us/documents/sb19181/Overview/SB_19_181_Final.pdf

[38] Dan Elliott, "Colorado Governor Signs Major Overhaul of Oil and Gas Rules," AP NEWS (Associate Press, April 17, 2019), https://apnews.com/ca4a57d130b64c658901f4d4b773c9ab)

former Congressman Dr. Ron Paul. Libertarian organizations like SAFER and others led the campaign to legalize medical marijuana in 2008 and recreational marijuana in 2012. People forget many Gadsden "Don't Tread On Me" flags were flying at the legalization celebrations. In these years, the Ron Paul campaign remained prominent throughout the state. Libertarian Ron Paul carried 21 out of the 33 delegates sent to the national convention in 2012.[39] However, the fraud and manipulation within the Colorado GOP caucus at the hands of establishment Mitt Romney voters reminded many that the neoconservative faction still had a stranglehold on the state. Romney delegates went as low as copying Ron Paul delegate slate flyers to deceive the voters at the state convention.[40] As we all know, Mitt Romney eventually lost to President Obama in the 2012 general election. The corruption reached its peak in the Presidential election of 2016 when the Colorado GOP canceled the presidential straw poll vote in fear that Donald Trump may win. Proponents of the removal argued the change was due to a recent rule change at the national level that bound the caucus popular vote to individual delegates' votes.[41] Ironically, this rule change was in response to the Ron Paul movement. The state ended up voting for Ted Cruz, who lost to Trump. The situation resulted in a new state policy that allows independents and democrats to vote in a GOP primary, thereby opening the door to manipulation and cementing the Colorado GOP's destruction.

Colorado Sheriffs have truly done a terrible job protecting the 2nd amendment and Colorado's own constitutional gun rights amendment. The Jefferson County Sheriff's office and other reporting departments acted like cowards on April 20, 1999, in their 3-hour stand-down during the Columbine massacre. Since then, the elected sheriffs continue to support the 2nd amendment vocally while condemning the right to protect one's self, property, or another person in practice. Although more than

---

[39] Lynn Bartels, "Colorado Republicans Split Delegate Votes between Romney, Unified Paul and Santorum Supporters," The Denver Post (The Denver Post, May 2, 2016), https://www.denverpost.com/2012/04/14/colorado-republicans-split-delegate-votes-between-romney-unified-paul-and-santorum-supporters/)

[40] Anonymous 2012 Colorado Congressional Republican Delegate. Interview by H. Nicholas Scott. Phone Interview. Denver, CO. January 26th, 2020.

[41] John Frank, "Colorado Republicans Cancel Presidential Vote at 2016 Caucus," The Denver Post (The Denver Post, April 22, 2016), https://www.denverpost.com/2015/08/25/colorado-republicans-cancel-presidential-vote-at-2016-caucus/)

half of Colorado's sheriffs did not support the 15-round magazine restriction law passed in 2012[42], they have supported other unconstitutional gun restrictions since then. The felony menacing law directly inhibits the right to self-defense and has even created an entire insurance industry for legal defense. Many defense attorneys have argued that the law is being utilized as "de facto gun confiscation," due to the law's open-ended wording, which allows for multiple situations to be open to interpretation, depending on the opinion of the reporting officer:

1) A person commits the crime of menacing if, by any threat or physical action, he or she knowingly places or attempts to place another person in fear of imminent serious bodily injury. Menacing is a class 3 misdemeanor, but it is a class 5 felony if committed:

(a) By the use of a deadly weapon or any article used or fashioned in a manner to cause a person to reasonably believe that the article is a deadly weapon; or

(b) By the person representing verbally or otherwise that he or she is armed with a deadly weapon.[43]

One would presume that if you are defending yourself, the goal would be to place the person threatening you "in fear of imminent serious bodily injury." Without a doubt, this law has been infringing on individual property rights and gun rights for many years, and Colorado Republicans have remained silent. The "Red Flag" gun confiscation law is undeniably the most oppressive of Colorado's gun-rights restrictions. The law that instantly destroys due process merely with hearsay was endorsed by Douglas County Sheriff Tony Spurlock, a supposed Republican and "2nd amendment guy."[44] Colorado Sheriffs, especially the Republican ones (which is the majority of them), have proven time and again they cannot be trusted to protect Coloradans' 2nd amendment rights.

Overall, these situations reveal the core problem within

42 Joella Baumann, "Colorado Supreme Court To Decide Fate Of Ban On High-Capacity Magazines," Colorado Public Radio (Colorado Public Radio, July 1, 2019), https://www.cpr.org/2019/04/23/colorado-supreme-court-to-decide-fate-of-ban-on-high-capacity-magazines/

43 CRS Title 18. Criminal Code § 18-3-206.

44 Jaclyn Allen, "Sheriff: Bill Could Have Saved Deputy's Life," The Denver Channel (KMGH, April 24, 2018), https://www.thedenverchannel.com/news/360/douglas-county-sheriff-red-flag-bill-could-have-saved-deputy-parrishs-life)

the Republican Party, ignoring the will of its constituents. The GOP constituency has a strong streak of conservatism mixed with libertarianism. The GOP continues to vote along a neoconservative path, which argues for more war and policies with no regard for domestic spending. They have ignored the constituency's prominent concerns regarding illegal immigration and gun control, which has consequently led to a Democratic takeover of the state. The Colorado GOP focused its attention more on upholding the status quo while ignoring the voters' will instead of attacking the progressive policies that have led to the destruction of the state party and possibly the culture of the state itself.

Agenda 2030 & Colorado

Colorado is "ground-zero" for the implementation of the United Nations' Agenda 2030. The "Gang of Four" who financed Colorado's takeover have also pledged allegiance to the sustainable development movement. Ultimately, their political aspirations are in direct alignment with Agenda 2030 policy proposals, and all of their political action committees work with other nongovernmental organizations that support this UN plan directly. Multinational corporations have also put their sights on Colorado to profit from Agenda 2030. Why Colorado, and why now? In the end, Colorado was chosen for its natural proclivity for fostering the infrastructure of the United States, namely the federal workforce and the US military. In reality, Colorado is the political petri dish for the growth of Agenda 2030 nationwide and eventually worldwide. The regulatory concoction will be carried like a virus to each state, transforming the nation forever. To fully illustrate Agenda 2030's influence in Colorado, we must examine its early roots in the state.

The United Nations Agenda 2030 program has early beginnings in Colorado. In 1997, the City of Fort Collins was one of the first to sign on to the International Council for Local Environmental Initiatives' "climate protection" campaign. ICLEI was founded in 1990 by 200 local governments from 43 countries who met for the first World Congress of Local Governments for a Sustainable Future at the United Nations headquarters in

New York.[45] In essence, the organization serves as a sidearm operation for Agenda 2030. They both rely on the implementation of sustainable development protocols. Fort Collins is not the only city in Colorado to sign on to this plan; here is a full list of cities that have pledged their loyalty to ICLEI: Aspen, Boulder, Breckenridge, Denver, Durango, Eagle County, Edgewater, Jefferson County, Lakewood, Westminster.[46] The entire front range of Colorado has bowed down to the United Nations and its Agenda 2030 program.

Fort Collins and its sister city Loveland have successfully implemented regulatory policy from ICLEI and the United Nations. Both cities are members of ICLEI's sustainable development program. In the last twenty years, they have transformed the local infrastructure with drastic changes to land use and transportation. Multi-use apartment residential complexes have been consistently replacing what was once farmland or old single-family residential units. Bike lanes now impede vehicle traffic lanes everywhere throughout both cities. Corrupt business transactions for private land and property holdings follow each agreement made under the recommendations of ICLEI. All of this is being done under the guise of reducing their respective cities' carbon footprints. The City of Fort Collins has set the objective of reducing the city's greenhouse gas emissions by 80% by 2050.[47] Without a doubt, this will have a sizeable impact on the area's farming and industrial communities.

Since these changes, Fort Collins has risen to 3rd in the nation for cyclist traffic.[48] At the same time, Colorado has seen an increasing trend of cyclist accidents deaths in the last ten years. In 2018, 60 people were killed on their bikes alone. The overall perspective of city managers represents that of the academic community: "narrower traffic lanes mean slower speeds," says Wesley Marshall, an associate professor of civil engineering

[45] "Who We Are," Who is ICLEI | ICLEI Global, accessed March 19, 2020, http://old.iclei.org/index.php?id=8)

[46] "Our Local Government Members & Regional and Higher Education Affiliates," ICLEI USA, accessed March 19, 2020, https://icleiusa.org/membership/)

[47] "2010 Climate Action Plan Status Report" (City of Fort Collins, July 2011), https://www.fcgov.com/climateaction/pdf/2010CAPStatusReport.pdf?1509983351)

[48] Jacob Laxen, "Fort Collins Named Third Best Biking City in Nation," Coloradoan (The Coloradoan, October 11, 2018), https://www.coloradoan.com/story/life/2018/10/11/fort-collins-named-countrys-third-best-biking-city/1602373002/)

at the University of Colorado at Denver.[49] Unfortunately, it seems that cities would rather slow down vehicle traffic with narrow traffic lanes than adding protected bike lanes that serve everyone's interests. In the end, the goal is to change human behavior in these cities so that citizens are forced to live in "walkable communities" where driving is not only not necessary, it will be forbidden.

Corruption is an intrinsic part of the Agenda 2030/ ICLEI land development format. The public-private partnerships created out of each program recommendation has resulted in blatant corruption, mostly surrounding real estate transactions and land development. Rocky Mountain Innosphere is a private company that focuses on creating lease space for tech startups with help from the city of Fort Collins and approximately $3.4 million in loans. The company also has direct support from Colorado State University. The company's relationship with the city is a revolving door—their current CEO, Mike Freeman, was previously the Chief Financial Officer for the Fort Collins city government. Of course, they were able to secure an $18 million contract in 2017.[50] In Loveland, Colorado, the city has a relationship with the organization "Artspace," which invests in real estate development projects for "artists and creators." Loveland's Metropolitan planning department funnels tax dollars to this organization, and Artspace reaps all of the profit from each project. The Loveland Housing Authority does have financial input on the affordable housing options available at the development, including residential and commercial units with a designated space for "creating."[51] This type of arrangement between city and developer has repeated itself over and over again across the front range.[52] In Arvada, Colorado, the city council approved a $30

[49] Kailyn Lamb, "Safety Advocates Seek to Stop Bicycle Fatality Trend," Centennial Citizen (Colorado Community Media, September 3, 2019), https://centennialcitizen.net/stories/safety-advo-cates-seek-to-stop-bicycle-fatality-trend,285622)

[50] Pat Ferrier, "Innosphere Plans $18M Expansion in Fort Collins, Denver," Coloradoan (The Coloradoan, December 8, 2017), https://www.coloradoan.com/story/money/business/2017/12/08/innosphere-plans-18-m-expansion-fort-collins-denver/922755001/)

[51] "Artspace Loveland Arts Campus," Artspace, accessed March 19, 2020, https://www.artspace.org loveland#leasing-section)

[52] Stacy Lynne, "Plan Cheyenne Town Hall," Plan Cheyenne Town Hall, accessed March 1, 2020, https:/ www.youtube.com/watch?v=iEABMOFdqAc)

land deal in 2018 for an apartment complex.[53] Yes, you read that correctly—thirty dollars for land to build apartments in line with Agenda 2030 zoning standards. In essence, business deals create a monopoly for the developer and the government. No ownership options are ever offered in these zoning agreements—the residential options are always restricted to renting, not owning. This is mainly because ICLEI and Agenda 2030 call for affordable housing price controls.

A tent city on Logan Street in progressive Denver, Colorado.

While Colorado is experiencing a substantial boom in economic growth, housing options remain limited throughout the state. Mostly, Colorado's housing situation resembles what is occurring nationwide for states that have strong economies. Americans across the country are struggling to find affordable housing options due to a shortage of inventory, and homelessness rates have skyrocketed. In one area of the market, cities force developers to build luxury apartments and affordable housing options in sustainable development communities. Since legislators have failed to sign construction defect legislation that will induce developers to build condos and townhomes in Colorado, devel-

---

[53] Dave Chandler, "Mr. Mayor, It's Still a $30 Land Deal," Arvada Press (Colorado Community Media, June 12, 2018), https://arvadapress.com/stories/mr-mayor-its-still-a-30-land-deal,263318)

opers are only building these two residential products in metro-politan areas. In suburban areas, developers are only building large single-family homes, which do not alleviate the middle to lower class sectors of the market. We are witnessing a complete restructuring of Colorado's economy at the hands of Agenda 2030 conspirators looking to create legalized monopolies with the government's help.

Corrupt development deals mandate "sustainable living" in Denver's plan for microapart-ments (600 sq ft or less).

Denver, the next Mega-Smart-City

The sustainable development agenda is the main driver for the trendy "smart city" initiatives that have recently been promoted by corporations like Verizon and AT&T, as they will be some of the main benefactors of this plan. It is no surprise that Denver has been selected as one of the main cities for the US Department of Transportation's "Smart City Challenge" because Denver is a "city whose progressive approach to innovation is rooted in its pioneering, Western spirit."[54] Quite the misnomer as Agenda 2030 is designed to destroy what is left of the American West. In reality, the United Nations smart city agenda is

---

[54] Denver Smart City, accessed March 19, 2020, https://www.denvergov.org/content/denvergov/en/denver-smart-city.html)

nowhere different from the mega-cities of the late 19th and early 20th centuries in New York and Chicago. These concepts are not original; they have simply been rebranded to remove the concept of individual property ownership altogether.

The smart city agenda developed by the US government and multinational corporations is the Agenda 2030 program's foundation. The program requires extensive monitoring and data collection, which will require extensive infrastructure. In July of 2019, Denver was selected by the CTIA (Cellular Telecommunications and Internet Association) for the meeting location for the Smart Cities Business and Technology Working Group to discuss how to "develop tools and resources that will increase efficiencies, promote collaboration and drive economic growth for municipalities across the country." The two-day meeting focused on the critical elements of building a smart city and some of its benefits:

- Building **large data centers** for companies like EdgeMicro and Flexential to handle the data traffic necessary to maintain a smart city.
- **5G networks** will be integral to a smart city's infrastructure to maintain real-time decision-making activities like emergency response communications, vehicle communications, and wireless networks. Companies like Arrow Civil, Black & Veatch, and Comptek have "perfected the process of installing 5G poles with Colorado's streamlined permitting process for small cell infrastructure."
- Business leaders looked at power solutions such as high-efficiency solar panels and transportation options such as autonomous shuttle vans and personal vehicles. [55]

The entire smart city framework is designed to increase maximum efficiency under the guise of reducing carbon footprints, greenhouse gases, and traffic. It is the main utility for Agenda 2030 and ICLEI's objectives. Panasonic's "Vehicle-to-Everything (V2X)" Operations Center processes data for one of the largest Connected Vehicle (CV) projects in North America, which spans 90 miles between Golden and Vail,

[55] "How the Mile-High City Is Embracing Smart City Solutions," CTIA, accessed March 19, 2020, https://www.ctia.org/news/how-the-mile-high-city-is-embracing-smart-city-solutions)

CO.[56] The system transmits data ten times per second, providing enough information to "make informed traffic and safety decisions." In reality, the system represents the ultimate control grid to ensure you are not exceeding your carbon footprint limits. Cities will be built so that a ban on personal vehicles would be enforced with a computer keystroke. Without a doubt, the Smart City agenda is a direct assault on individual liberty and personal autonomy.

Verizon, other corporations, and nongovernmental organizations have selected Denver as one of twenty other cities[57] to roll out this program that will eventually be implemented nationwide per Agenda 2030 standards. When considering Denver's geographical location and the vital role the Federal government has given it, it is clear that Denver plays a much more pivotal role when compared to those other cities.

For the United Nations Agenda 2030 political and economic plans to be effective, there must be a central hub for its implementation. In the United Nations' Agenda 2030, cities like Washington DC and the United Nations' home in New York will be the primary source of control. However, Denver should be perceived as the "2nd capital of the United States." Colorado's important role for national defense has provided for the perfect infrastructure for the rollout of Agenda 2030, as these technology firms work heavily with the defense industry. That is precisely why the United Nations' labeled Denver as one of the next "mega-cities," Denver will be the central hub that connects them all. At the time of the new international airport's construction and eventual completion in 1997, many questioned: "why? Why did Denver need such a large airport, when the one we had simply needed a renovation?" Now, the answer has become crystal-clear. According to the UN, Colorado will eventually hold one of the largest populations in the United States, and it will require an extensive transportation network. Recent plans have been announced to extend rail services from Fort Collins to Pueblo, with a hyper-loop train from the airport to the mountain ski resorts. Without a doubt, the elites have big plans for Colorado!

56 Ibid.

57 Verizon 5G Ultra Wideband service coming to Denver in 2019, accessed March 19, 2020, https://www. denvergov.org/content/denvergov/en/mayors-office/newsroom/2019/verizon-5g-ultra-wideband-service-coming-to-denver-in-2019.html)

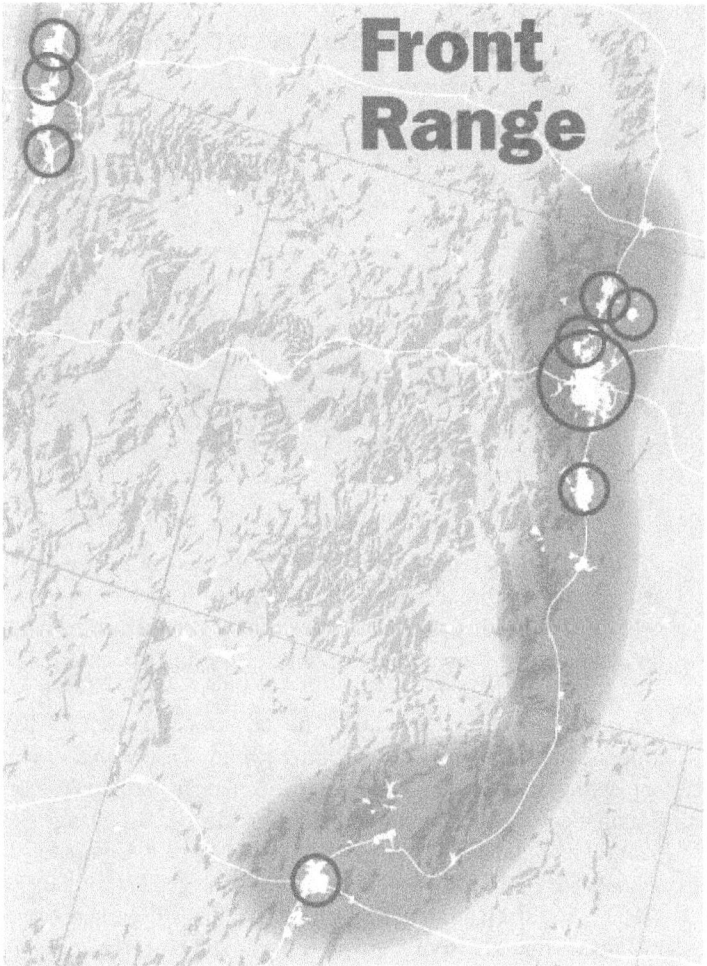

Figure (D) America 2050 Regional Planning Association's diagram for Megacity along the Front Range.

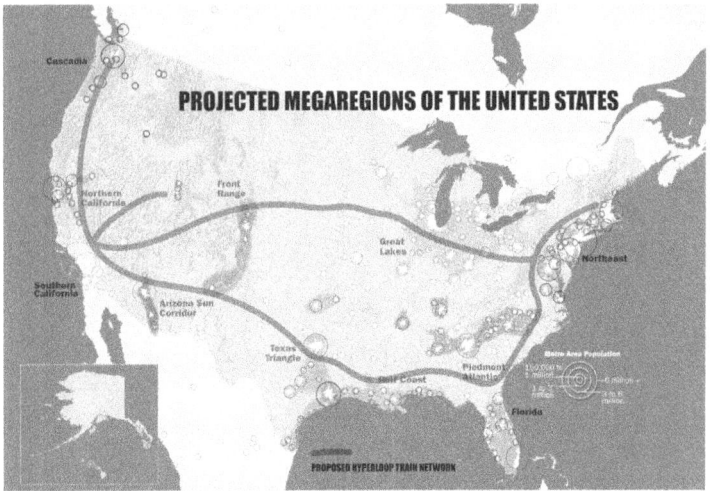

Figure (E) Projected Megaregions of the U.S., America 2050 Prospectus Report, Regional Planning Association. Hyperloop map based on multiple planned projects.

The Marxist takeover of Colorado was not by accident and represents a broader plan for the country. It was never considered possible that states that were once solidly red could be flipped blue in a short amount of time. California's transformation from a red state to a blue state took almost fifty years. How could this process be expedited? The transformation was a 3-step process: first, supplant a state's current voting base with a foreign one, while offering them access to the American welfare system. Simultaneously, the current voting base's ideals must change over time with the local school districts' assistance. Colorado schools have primarily become indoctrination centers for the socialist transformation of America. All of this will be supported by outside funding from political activists and business investors. The amount of outside funding poured into Colorado's elections for the last twenty years is unprecedented. This strategy was the key difference; previously, political donors focused on spreading their resources abroad while also focusing on local candidates in races that could be won. Now, the political victors from other states focus their attention on surrounding states as part of this broader plan with Agenda 2030.

Undoubtedly, the "Colorado Method" will be utilized

in other states at the hands of the Democratic party with the assistance from the Republicans with a coordinated stand-down. We have already seen this political process repeated in states like Virginia, Texas, Nevada, Idaho, Oregon, and Washington. Virginia is undeniably the best example of the efficacy of the Agenda 2030 platform; Democrats were able to take over the legislature in half the time it took in Colorado. Virginia Democrats have already passed a red flag gun law and a law that allows cities to ban certain weapons within city limits. They are going for broke—if passed, the gun control bills currently being debated in the Virginia legislature will be the most draconian laws the nation has ever seen. They are looking to pass universal background checks, gun registration, and an assault weapons ban. There are already rumblings of Idaho and Texas being flipped blue as they are also experiencing a demographic wave from progressive California. Idaho saw a 2.1% population increase in 2019, and the Democrats gained three seats in the statehouse in the 2018 election.[58] The population has grown by 1.25% down south in Texas, with most newcomers traveling from other states, namely California, New York, and Illinois. Texas has also seen an increase in Latino voter turnout and younger voter turnout, which bodes well for the socialists in the Democratic Party.[59]

California went from a state full of freedom-loving people to a state full of degenerate socialists because it allowed for the creation of a Marxist petri dish within its borders. Once California was conquered, it became the unofficial breeding ground for communist political activists looking to spread their cancer nationwide. The technocratic elites that transformed California knew that they had to increase their political efficiency in other states if they wanted to take over America. Colorado was the first political casualty of this takeover; the "Colorado Method" represents this political strategy, and Agenda 2030 is the endgame. One by one, each state will slowly begin to resemble California politically, culturally, and economically. The question at hand is: how do we stop the Californication of America?

[58] Keith Ridler, "Is Idaho Turning a Little Blue? Primary Might Provide Clues," AP NEWS (Associated Press, March 5, 2020), https://apnews.com/45486c6b90f7cae1b237248fef3f05bf)

[59] Ashley Lopez, "Super Tuesday Could Show Just How Blue Texas Is Turning," NPR (NPR, March 2, 2020), https://www.npr.org/2020/03/02/810401130/super-tuesday-could-show-just-how-blue-texas-is-turning)

VII

Tiny Solutions for Big Problems

In recent years, homelessness has become a serious problem for America. Every major city in America has pockets of systemic poverty, some larger than others. This chapter's main objective is to illustrate the direct relationship between the homeless population and the lack of available housing options. Simultaneously, we will show that private property rights are essential to reestablishing other natural rights in America. The first step to reclaiming the Bill of Rights is to rebuild its core foundation with the original concepts of individual sovereignty and private property rights. Finally, we will look at the necessary solutions to America's housing crisis, which will help resurrect individual liberty's central tenets throughout the country. The concept of private property must be restored to thwart the establishment of an American technocracy under Agenda 2030.

In the last ten years, the United States' chronic homeless population has decreased by approximately 16 percent or approximately 17,000 people to approximately 106,250.[1] However, when examining the data, it becomes clear that there are other problems at hand. Roughly two-thirds of this population lives outdoors or in abandoned buildings.[2] There is no denying that the Obama administration worked hard to curb chronic homelessness rates throughout the country, with the total amount of homeless people declining from 650,000 in 2007 to 564,000 in 2015. Unfortunately, the type of housing they are receiving ultimately leads to an endless cycle of dependence on the government. The chart below shows that the rate of chronic homelessness is decreasing because more people are being supported by government housing.

---

[1] Meghan Henry et al., "The 2018 Annual Homeless Assessment Report (AHAR) to Congress" (The U.S. Department of Housing and Urban Development, December 2018), https://files.hudexchange.info/resources/documents/2018-AHAR-Part-1.pdf, p.4)

[2] Ibid.

Figure 10. Number of People Living in Emergency Shelter and Transitional Housing in the United States, 2007–18

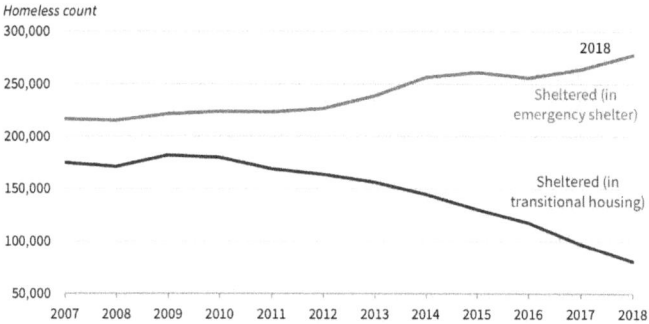

Figure (A) Shelter Chart from Whitehouse Report on Homelessness in America, September 2019.

This data does not accurately depict the overall health of the housing market; it only represents a small part of the overall picture.

Nevertheless, the data accurately shows that the rate of homelessness is increasing in America. In reality, more people are being brought off the streets into government housing, which is not a healthy solution for the American people. It represents the endgame for the Agenda 2030 future economy, where there is no longer a middle class, but a large swath of the population who will always be dependent on the government or a corporation for their housing needs, among other things.

When looking at the homeless situation in cities across the country, it is no surprise that Los Angeles, California, and New York City lead the entire pack.[3] Both of these cities are notorious for having highly ineffective and expensive housing markets. Other cities like Boston, Massachusetts, and Chicago, Illinois, also made the list. Is it simply a case of the effects of living in a large population center? Or, is it a case of poor development planning, which has led to inefficiencies in the market?

[3] "The State of Homelessness in America," The State of Homelessness in America § (2019), https://www.whitehouse.gov/wp-content/uploads/2019/09/The-State-of-Homelessness-in-America.pdf, p.1)

147

Figure 2. Overall Homeless Population by State, 2018

Number of people experiencing
homelessness per 10,000 people

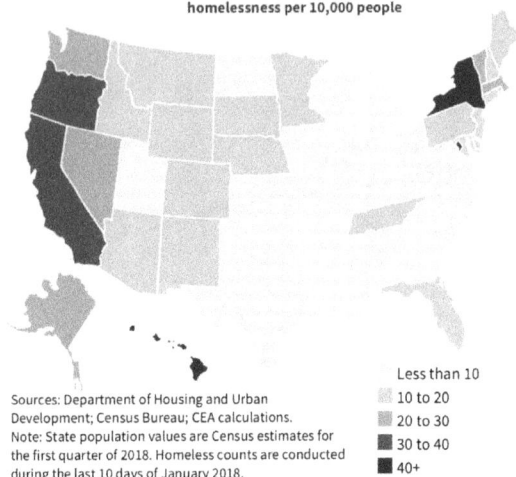

Sources: Department of Housing and Urban
Development; Census Bureau; CEA calculations.
Note: State population values are Census estimates for
the first quarter of 2018. Homeless counts are conducted
during the last 10 days of January 2018.

Less than 10
10 to 20
20 to 30
30 to 40
40+

Figure (B) Map of Homeless Population in America, Whitehouse Report on Homelessness, September 2019.

In all of these big cities, their leaders believe that the best way to attack homelessness and high housing prices is to provide government-subsidized housing and emergency homeless shelters. At the same time, politicians are working with developers to build more apartments, arguing that this will help with the inventory shortages that exist in almost every city and state. Unfortunately for tenants and buyers, an increased emphasis on apartment building has led to a decrease in condominiums and single-family starts, which promote individual ownership. According to current government data, multifamily units zoned for rent comprise 96% of new construction starts.[4] This would explain the increasing rent burden most Americans have to live with each month as more people are forced into rental situations, where demand still outpaces supply. According to The Pew Charitable Trusts, the share of severely rent-burdened renter households—spending 50 percent or more of monthly income on rent—increased by 42 percent between 2001 and 2015, to 17

---

[4] Robert Dietz, "Multifamily Construction Data: 2nd Quarter 2019," Eye On Housing, August 19, 2019, http://eyeonhousing.org/2019/08/multifamily-construction-data-2nd-quarter-2019/)

percent [of all rental households].[5] The only way to reduce rental prices is to decrease the demand by inducing these potential renters into becoming potential buyers.

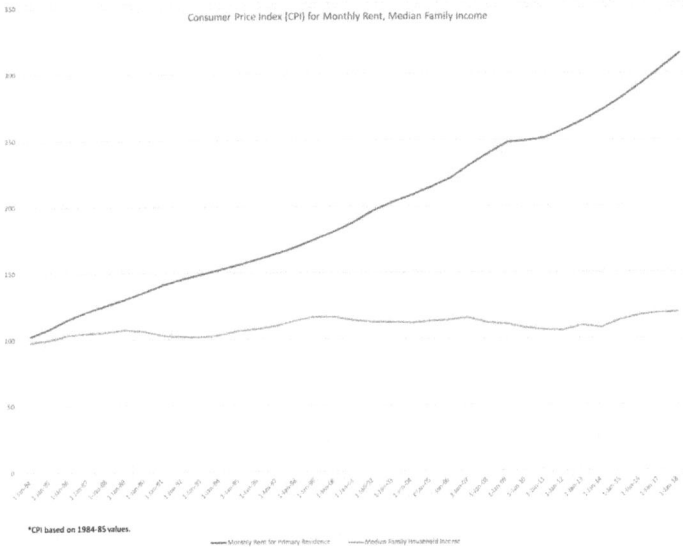

Consumer Price Index (CPI) for Monthly Rent, Median Family Income

*CPI based on 1984-85 values.

Monthly Rent for Primary Residence   Median Family Household Income

Figure (C) CPI for Monthly Rent, Median Family Income. Data Source: St. Louis Fed.

When comparing this data with the United Nations' Agenda 2030 program's stated objectives, the implications are alarming. It is clear that America's current housing market failures do not merely represent the mistakes of misinformed politicians and building developers, but a cohesive plan developed by the global economic elite and proponents of the Agenda 2030 initiative. Americans are quickly becoming permanent renters: more U.S. households are renting now than at any point in the last 50

5 "American Families Face a Growing Rent Burden," The Pew Charitable Trusts, accessed April 12, 2020, https://www.pewtrusts.org/en/research-and-analysis/reports/2018/04/american-families-face-a-growing-rent-burden)

years.[6] The data is undeniable: the American housing market is being transformed into a permanent rental economy.

The solutions to fix the American housing market are simple when viewing the economy from an Austrian economics perspective. In short, Austrian economic theory argues that the functions of the free market, namely supply and demand, will always remain constant no matter the attempts to influence it. When governments decide that building more government-subsidized housing will help alleviate high prices in the market, the proponents of Austrian economic theory would argue that these governments are artificially increasing the supply of housing units at a lower price, which does not alleviate demand for purchases. Why? It is all about the incentives. The 2018 White House study on homelessness in America notes that:

> Expanding the supply of homeless shelters and government-subsidized housing shifts the demand for homes inward and increases homelessness. A larger shelter supply entails a higher shelter quality (i.e., characteristics of a shelter that make it more desirable as a place to stay) at any given number of beds. Mandating a right-to-shelter with a sufficiently high minimum quality level could thus substantially increase sheltered homeless populations.[7]

This logic also applies to government-subsidized rent with Section 8 housing programs. For most people, government housing is not desirable. You cannot alter the building in any way. You do not have control over the price of rent, and the government can withdraw your voucher. This market area attracts those who may be accepting other forms of government welfare, which inevitably breeds lazy behavior and criminal activity. In other words, those living in government housing are always looking to get out—the effect on the demand for housing in the private market is nullified. The other side effect is that the welfare class becomes comfortable with government housing, and willfully chooses not to enter the private sector, which also puts pressure on the housing market. This leaves the "free" housing market to

[6] Anthony Cilluffo, A.W. Geiger, and Richard Fry, "More U.S. Households Are Renting than at Any Point

in 50 Years," Pew Research Center (Pew Research Center, July 19, 2017), https://www.pewresearch.org/fact-tank/2017/07/19/more-u-s-households-are-renting-than-at-any-point-in-50-years/)

[7] "The State of Homelessness in America," The State of Homelessness in America § (2019), https://www.whitehouse.gov/wp-content/uploads/2019/09/The-State-of-Homelessness-in-America.pdf, p. 6)

live in a separate market on its own, which is now more limited due to the government's ownership stake in the market.

When viewing the housing market from this perspective, the best route to alleviate housing prices is to increase the supply of units for purchase. "True supply" equates to single-family units and multifamily units available for private sale and do not belong to any affordable housing program. This is where most people want to participate in the market, where they own a financial stake in their future. For most, ownership is preferable to renting as it allows for full control of the property and the expected cost of living. For those that do like the ease of renting, the quality of rentals would increase due to the fact more people can easily own their home; fewer people renting equates to less demand, which leads to lower prices. Former Congressman and Presidential candidate Ron Paul asserts in his book *Liberty Defined:*

> [The Austrian School] provides a way of looking at economics that takes into account the unpredictability of human action (absolutely no one can quantitatively know the future) and the vital role of human choice in the way economies work (in markets, consumers drive decisions overproduction), and explains how it is that order can emerge out of the seeming chaos of individual action.[8]

The constant game the government plays in the housing market by increasing supply in some areas and decreasing it in others leads to constant market imbalances, which leads to volatile housing booms and busts.

It is undeniable that if city leaders truly wanted to alleviate housing prices, they would not be engaging in shady development deals, such as the $30 land deal in Arvada, Colorado, for more expensive luxury apartments, instead of condominiums or townhomes for individual sale. They would not be building more affordable housing units, where tenants become more addicted to government intervention with no positive effect on the housing market. And finally, they would not be incentivizing false homeownership where someone buys a property that has deed restrictions on the price it can be sold for later. These scenarios are called "permanent affordable housing," where the home's

[8] Ron Paul, Liberty Defined: the 50 Essential Issues That Affect Our Freedom (New York: Grand Central, 2012), p.17)

151

price is always gauged by government officials. This scenario was alarming for some misinformed homeowners in Denver, Colorado, where they were shocked to find out they could not sell the home for its actual value, typically tens of thousands of dollars more than the restricted price Denver had mandated the property be sold for. With this program, if you earn more money than the program allows, you will be forced out of your home.[9] These mandates will have a ripple effect on the market; it will artificially lower home prices in the surrounding area, which will increase demand from homeowners who would usually not have access to the market.

The artificially induced attempts to alleviate the housing market by the government tend to have the exact opposite intended effect. If they genuinely wanted to relieve housing prices, they would simply zone for more inventory and incentivize builders to do what they do best. Ultimately, city leaders and developers should work to build comprehensive products that address all areas of the local market. If there are market imbalances, the problem should always be addressed at the level where private sales occur. What other ways does the government negatively impact the housing market?

Arbitrary and oppressive zoning requirements have created false scarcity in the U.S. housing market. Some of the most restrictive regulations are those that demand minimum square footage requirements for new home construction. In most states, it is simply impossible to put a small home on private land. Most minimum square footages for detached properties start at 2000 square feet. Likewise, cities and towns have disallowed putting a recreational vehicle on private property. In Colorado, residents cannot have an RV on private land for actual use for more than five months in any county. All of these restrictions limit housing options at the lower end of the economic spectrum.

The regulations surrounding the construction and maintenance of new buildings have also added significant housing market costs. The National Association of Homebuilders reports that government regulations account for roughly 24 percent of

---

[9] "People in Denver Forced to Sell Affordable Housing They Didn't Know They Bought," KUSA, March 21, 2018, https://www.9news.com/article/news/local/next/people-in-denver-forced-to-sell-affordable-housing-they-didnt-know-they-bought/73-530761758)

building costs for single-family homes.[10] Likewise, a similar report found that regulations account for approximately 30 percent of building costs with multifamily properties.[11] Sure, many of these regulations are valuable and necessary, such as restrictions on the size of stairwells and egress for fire safety, among others. However, regulations that focus on energy efficiency have become the main source of headaches for developers and builders alike.

Finally, some of the oppression we experience as homeowners is because we entered into a voluntary contract with our neighbors to maintain certain community elements. Homeowner's associations can be the primary source of pain for many homeowners if they are being mismanaged. If finances are not maintained, HOA costs can skyrocket. If the physical property is not maintained, costly assessments could bankrupt a homeowner. Homeowners need to understand these risks and the negative caveats of entering into such a contract. If property rights and privacy matter to you, entering into an association-managed community may not be the best option. For the most part, there is no recourse through government intervention, which would likely make the situation worse. Litigation is often the only resort or avoiding the situation altogether by purchasing a detached property on private land.

Solutions

Government's role in the housing market

Without a doubt, the violent economic swings that we have seen in the last thirty years in the housing markets have had the most substantial impact on Americans' standard of living. These recessions and depressions directly result from the Federal Reserve artificially pumping up the market with low-interest rates and local governments buying up properties for affordable housing units. All government intervention in the market results

---

[10] Paul Emrath, "Government Regulation in the Price of a New Home," NAHB (National Association of Homebuilders, May 2, 2016), https://www.nahbclassic.org/generic.aspx?genericContentID=250611)

[11] Paul Emrath and Caitlin Walter, "Regulation: Over 30 Percent of the Cost of a Multifamily Development"(National Association of Homebuilders, June 2018), https://www.nmhc.org/contentassets/60365ef-fa073432a8a168619e0f30895/nmhc-nahb-cost-of-regulations.pdf)

in the opposite of the intended effect. The Federal government should rely on a national banking system that lets the market determine interest rates. Local governments should allow housing prices to fluctuate in the market without their intervention with unnecessary price controls. The government should play the role of the referee; it cannot be both referee and player. Continuing with this analogy, the government should essentially set up different games for everyone to play in. There should be designated housing developments for all consumers to be able to participate in the market. Whether someone is rich, middle-class, or poor, they should have access to private property. Developers can easily be incentivized to build these types of products. Ultimately, zoning for the people and corporations alike will lead to a truly balanced market, which should be the main goal.

Kicking Agenda 2030 & ICLEI to the curb

The power grabs from the EPA and the BLM in the name of the United Nations 2030 agenda have restricted access to lands, consequently squeezing the market. Many people value the national and state park systems; however, the Feds now have a monopoly over the states with land control and have clearly shown their willingness to abuse their power. To restore proper land rights for the individual, the federal government must restore land control to the states.

Simultaneously, American citizens need to take control of their local city councils and reject any existing and new partnerships with ICLEI and any organizations similar to it. These organizations recommend that cities yield their control to multinational corporations looking to profit from the new rental economy. The sustainable development programs have shown that they restrict ease of access and increase businesses' costs while stripping citizens of their private property rights. Instead of signing on to plans that uphold a specific preconceived agenda, city councils should report to their constituents for input on development and city planning.

Curbing government regulations in housing construction, the role of NGOs

Organizations like the National Association of Home-builders and other local organizations consistently work toward curbing unnecessary costs and burdens from arbitrary government regulations. Nevertheless, many have been quick to comply with codes that are there to enforce the corrupt Agenda 2030 sustainability structure. Homeowners should demand more control over what goes inside their homes, specifically things like smart meters and unnecessary add-ons that support the sustainable development movement's addiction to data tracking. Generally, homeowners want to have an energy-efficient home—it saves them money and keeps the house warm and cool as they desire. There is a difference between energy-efficient and sustainable. The term sustainable implies that the home was built with certain products to "protect the environment" when there may be other available products that are less expensive on the market. If the recommended change in behavior or product is based on hyperbole in the first place, it may be unnecessary. Recommendations made from NGOs like the International Building Code Council should be scrutinized before consideration. In the end, consumers have become complacent and willingly accept and, most times, even invite tyranny into their home.

Condominiums and Townhomes

With most multifamily construction starts in America being designated as rental properties, single and low-income earners now have one less ownership option available to them on the market. If you are lucky enough to find a condo or townhome for sale, they are often older properties, an example of people's options during a better time. Whether it is arbitrary litigation filed against builders and developers for building condos or zoning that creates rental monopolies, legislators, city leaders, and lobbyists must work toward opening up the market for a liberated America.

Tiny Homes

For the housing market to be balanced, the supply must meet all consumers' demands, no matter their income. That means someone that makes minimum wage at McDonald's should be able to afford a home. "What?!" That is the reaction most have today when hearing that statement. Those having that reaction are not seeing the possibilities that exist with some wood and a few tools. Square footage restrictions exist to maximize tax revenue and to allow a monopoly over low-income housing from the government. We build small homes on wheels with recreational vehicles, yet we do not allow a similar-sized home to be built on private land. The tiny home movement offers serious promise for shoring up housing for low-income families. However, there is a caveat to this recommendation: the home's land must be privately owned. This will allow full exposure to the housing market with all of the included benefits, namely, curing homelessness in America.

But, once again, the government has gotten in the way. For tiny homes to be built on private land, cities and towns must cease enforcing arbitrary minimum square footage laws that force homeowners to build larger houses. It is evident that cities see tiny homes and RVs as equitable housing; they have no problem zoning for tiny home rental communities, which allow the landowner to have tiny homes and RVs on their property, as long as they remain mobile and never hold land rights. Towns like Woodland Park, Colorado, would rather have an owner hold a large taxable amount of land with taxable rentable income than a bunch of individual plots that are taxed at much lower rates due to the small size of the home sitting on it. It always comes down to money and power.

Living a genuinely sustainable life

According to Austrian economic theory, to maintain balance within the market on a macro level, businesses and governments must operate within their budget. This rule applies to individuals as well. America's current economic structure is based purely on consumerism, where the government, corporations, and individuals live in a world of debt. Americans live paycheck-to-paycheck buying goods they really do not need. In America:

- Approximately 78% of us live paycheck-to-paycheck.[12]
- Only 40 percent of Americans have enough savings for a $1000 emergency.[13]
- Approximately 1/3 of us eat a fast-food meal every day.[14]
- We are on food stamps and also own Xboxes, PlayStations, tablets, and multiple cars.
- We live in Section 8 government housing and continue to have children.
- We reward people on welfare who have children with continued tax benefits. They continue to have children.

The American mindset must change. America was once known for a culture of self-reliance and hard work.

The 2008 recession and the 2020 COVID-19 pandemic revealed that not only did Americans not prepare for another financial crisis, but we also do not even know to prioritize food in the pantry. The 2008 recession robbed Americans of their retirement, and it would only be 12 years later that the same generations would be hit again with the fallout of the COVID-19 pandemic. For the first time in 100 years, food security became a serious issue in America, seemingly overnight. Production supply lines were instantly hit with exponential demand due to the fact Americans failed to stockpile food before the crisis and due to multiple virus-related deaths at food plants across the country.[15] The problem of empty shelves across America is no longer an unimaginable nightmare, it is now a reality.

We must work to become a self-reliant nation again. First, we must learn the principles of sound money with the Austrian economic theory. The rule is simple: only spend what you earn minus a personal tax for your savings account. Second, we must work to rely less on large systems for our sustenance.

[12] Zack Friedman, "78% Of Workers Live Paycheck To Paycheck," Forbes (Forbes Magazine, January 11, 2019), https://www.forbes.com/sites/zackfriedman/2019/01/11/live-paycheck-to-paycheck-government-shutdown/)

[13] AnnieReporter, "A $1,000 Emergency Would Push Many Americans into Debt," CNBC (CNBC, January 23, 2019), https://www.cnbc.com/2019/01/23/most-americans-dont-have-the-savings-to-cover-a-1000-emergency.html)

[14] Cheryl Fryar, Jeffrey Hughes, and Kirsten Herrick, "Fast Food Consumption Among Adults in the United States, 2013–2016" (CDC, National Center for Health Statistics, October 2018), https://www.cdc.gov/nchs/data/databriefs/db322-h.pdf)

[15] Josh Funk, "Virus Closes Some Meat Plants, Raising Fears of Shortages," AP NEWS (Associated Press, April 13, 2020), https://apnews.com/d855667c811d3d9810883e05702288ad)

As we have seen, America's food production line is susceptible to any type of disruption. Fast food and groceries that require no preparation from the consumer have made us dependent on this system. Americans must learn how to grow and store their food for the short term and the long term. How can we accomplish these goals? The tools for self-reliance can be found in the benefits and rights gained by owning property.

The Agenda 2030 model dictates that property owners must be contained within large cities with a "sustainable infrastructure" if one can own any property at all. That privilege will only be available to the technocratic elite. We know what this structure looks like with Agenda 2030. What structure represents the antithesis to the technocratic elite's plan? How should a home be built to resist the technocracy?

Let us build a home that the average single American could own to avert the technocratic feudalism that strips individuals of their right to live a truly sustainable and self-reliant life. The Agenda 2030 "smart home" is built so that its occupants are dependent on the system, or "the grid." Homeowners are dependent on the city for water and electricity and will have all of their usage data tracked and recorded. On the contrary, the Agenda 2030 "Liberty Home" will consist of systems that support ownership of everything within the walls of the home, including the water and energy that makes it suitable for living. Instead of submitting solar power to the grid, homes should store the energy on-site for later use. Instead of depending solely on city water, homes could build rainwater collection systems or work to obtain water rights if it is an option. If private land is not an option, developers could include these amenities as part of their plan for new homes, where homes can rely on the city if the sun is not shining while also storing energy.

Figure (D) Artist rendition of an elevation for the "Liberty Home."

Many homeowner's associations have restricted access for gardening and the use of farm animals on private land The Liberty Home would need to be built where growing large amounts of food is allowable where chickens, goats, and other livestock would be allowed to roam freely. In essence, modern society needs to adopt a modern version of the family farm, albeit on a smaller level. One should be able to grow their food or butcher their meat on their property. Likewise, someone who works full time could grow a large garden with little maintenance. If a private land plot is not an option, homeowner's associations and developers could create a sustainable condominium or townhome development with a community garden for local food access.

The concept of private property extends from the philosophical belief that every man is entitled to the fruits of his labor. By forfeiting our private information and data to the government and third-party corporations, we are ultimately sacrificing our private property rights. Our addiction to technology and convenience has enabled tyrants to steal our freedom. For every inch we give the technocrats, they continue to take a mile. Will we allow the capacity of computer technology to surpass our capacity for humanity? To effectively resist the technocratic takeover, we must take control of our private data and stop using oppressive applications. It is time that people disconnect from time-wasting technologies that reduce our ability to interact with one another and reconnect with their families, friends, and neighbors. As Simon Sinek says, we are dopamine addicts who cannot let go of our phones. It is time to kick the habit!

Any person can adopt this lifestyle, no matter their income or situation, as long as the government stays out of the way. The Liberty Home should be a home that matches one's income and lifestyle. If people enjoy living a simple life without many things, they should have access to that lifestyle without unnecessary square footage restrictions on the size of their home. If people want to live in an RV or a tiny home on a private plot of land, they should be able to do so. Otherwise, the laws force them to live unsustainable and inefficient lifestyles sacrificing their individual liberty and privacy in the process.

In the end, a truly sustainable lifestyle is one that adheres to the concept that every man is entitled to the fruits of his labor, which comes in the form of private property. To stop the technocratic takeover of America, complex Constitutional changes must occur on the national level. Before that happens, Americans must take back control of their country from the ground-up. We must take responsibility for our lifestyles and return to a culture of self-reliance before it is too late. By taking control of our land, our property, our transportation, our food, our health, and our data, we can regain the political power that we handed over to multinational corporations who are hell-bent on destroying the American way of life.

VIII

Back to the Constitution: The Answer to *1984* is *1776*!

"Government cannot create a world without risks, nor would we
really wish to live in such a fictional place."
Ron Paul, 2012

Property rights will continue to wane if the core principles of the Constitution continue to be ignored. We can only do so much as citizens under the current structure to protect these rights before our rights are gone completely. We can fight arbitrary HOA restrictions, property confiscation, and other functions of government overreach with attorneys and activism. In reality, we must attack the source of the problem at its root cause; otherwise, there will not be any path to defend property rights in court once the precedent is set. There is not a one-off solution to the multiple crises that America is currently experiencing; a complex problem requires complex solutions. Property rights and our definition of natural rights are under attack from multiple fronts: spiritually, philosophically, politically, and economically.

To manage these crises, we must examine our relationships with each other and the government. In reality, these relationships are one and the same. Our understanding of government is akin to our understanding of our rights as individuals and our relationship with our neighbors. To begin the healing process for America, we must take back our property rights and individual rights. We must expose any political factions that are waging war against our core principles through the use of cultural Marxism, which is antithetical to the laws of nature and mankind. In doing so, the core structure of the sustainable development movement and Agenda 2030 will fall apart. Finally, we must dismantle fraudulent institutions and unconstitutional bureaucracies. By removing the cancerous growth that is the heavy hand of government, Americans' creative power will be unleashed once again.

161

"Do to others as you would have them do to you." Who would think that the solution to all of our problems is contained in one bible verse? If we executed our political and legal system in this manner, the rights of man would remain paramount. The legal interpretation of what constitutes "tort law" is based on this same premise:

noun
LAW
    noun: **tort**; plural noun: **torts**
1.   a wrongful act or an infringement of a right (other than under contract) leading to civil legal liability.[1]

The Founding Fathers also shared this philosophy in their attempt to create a strong republic with the United States. Looking further, the origination of tort law has its roots with property law. An injury to one's self or one's property is an injury against one's liberty. James Madison states it best in Federalist No. 10:

The diversity in the faculties of men, from which the rights of property originate, is not less an insuperable obstacle to a uniformity of interests. The protection of these faculties is the first object of government. From the protection of different and unequal faculties of acquiring property, the possession of different degrees and kinds of property immediately results; and from the influence of these sentiments and the views of the respective proprietors ensues a division of society into different interests and parties.[2]

Any government's goal is to facilitate these types of voluntary contracts among men to maintain a stable, orderly society. Our differences should be respected and allowed to breathe through the free-market faculties, with the government playing the role of referee.

---

[1] *Oxford English Dictionary*. 3rd Edi. Oxford: Oxford University Press, 2020.

[2] James Madison, The Federalist Papers, No. 10, (Mineola, NY: Dover Publications, 2014), p.42)

When voluntary contracts are violated, an injury as occurred. According to Madison, if there is a perpetual environment in a society of negating and ignoring voluntary contracts between men, the division of society disintegrates. Unfortunately, America has fallen into crisis due to the fact it has ignored the core principles for which our government was founded: natural laws that have always governed the minds of men. As the government has gotten larger public willingness to adopt socialist and communist programs has increased. The core principles and values of the communists directly conflict with the concepts of tort law and the "golden rule." Their entire system is based upon theft. If we look at the communist manifesto again, we find that America may already have reached its destination to socialist hell:

1. **Abolition of property in land and application of all rents of land to public purposes**.
    - We have highlighted the lawless attempts by the Bureau of Land Management and other government agencies to confiscate and transfer land in the name of environmentalism or some other progressive cause.
    - We have highlighted the consistent attack on property rights through the use of abusive agreements between developers and the government and the tyrannical zoning restrictions that come with it.
    - We have highlighted that all of these actions have been taken to build a new social and economic order under the United Nations' Agenda 2030.
2. **A heavy progressive or graduated income tax.**
    - The current Democrat platform argues for heavy individual income taxes, corporate income taxes, and carbon taxes under Agenda 2030.
3. **Abolition of all right of inheritance.**
    - We have seen the repeated accusations from Democrats that there is too much "white privilege" in America. In reality, this is a front for destroying individual wealth for everyone with death taxes. Legislators in California have argued for a "white privilege

163

tax" or "reparations for slavery."[3]

4. **Confiscation of the property of all emigrants and rebels.**
   - According to the National Immigration Law Center, "HUD-funded programs that provide emergency shelter and transitional housing (for up to two years) are available to all immigrants, regardless of immigration status, so long as these programs do not consider income in determining eligibility."[4] It has been demonstrated that government housing programs lead to dependency, not actual property ownership. Eventually, Agenda 2030 will ensure property ownership will never be available to these groups—this will only be allowed for those that belong to the technocracy.
   - The Bundy Ranch, Oregon stand-offs with the Bureau of Land Management over the agency's unconstitutional land grabs highlight the brute force the government is willing to use to take land from American citizens.

5. **Centralization of credit in the hands of the state, by means of a national bank with state capital and an exclusive monopoly.**
   - The 16th Amendment of the Constitution authorized the private Federal Reserve to control the national economy and handle the issuing of credit for the U.S. government.

6. **Centralization of the means of communication and transport in the hands of the state.**
   - The Agenda 2030 outline for transportation mandates a heavy reliance on public transportation as personal transportation is relegated to a rental economy.
   - Facebook, Twitter, and other social media networks are designed to work hand-in-glove with the government to wield the heavy hand of censorship against dissenting Americans. The centralized network has allowed the alphabet agencies to document the rela-

[3] Associated Press DON THOMPSON, "California Moves to Consider Reparations for Slavery," SFGate, August 30, 2020, |PAGE|, accessed September 02, 2020, https://www.sfgate.com/news/article/California-moves-to-consider-reparations-for-15524833.php)

[4] Rental Housing Programs, report, October 2018, P.1 accessed September 2, 2020, https://www.nilc.org/wp-content/uploads/2016/03/rental_housing_1005.pdf)

164

tionships and activities of every American citizen.

7. **Extension of factories and instruments of production owned by the state; the bringing into cultivation of wastelands, and the improvement of soil generally in accordance with a common plan.**
   - Multiple government agencies have guidance in this arena, namely the BLM and EPA.
   - The environmental/sustainable development movement is the main driver for the Agenda 2030 program.
   - Multiple government bureaucracies regulate the agricultural industry.

8. **Equal liability of all to labor. Establishment of industrial armies, especially for agriculture.**
   - All proceeds from individual labor belong to the state. As Americans paychecks continue to grow smaller to pay for those not contributing, this statement becomes more accurate every day.
   - The Agenda 2030 land development protocols call for specific controls over land use and allocation.
   - The 2008 government bailout of the automotive industry and the regulation that comes with it mirrors the communist industrial army plan in function.

9. **Combination of agriculture with manufacturing industries; gradual abolition of the distinction between town and country, by a more equable distribution of the population over the country.**
   - The Washington Post reported in 2014 that from 1935 to 2000, America had seen a decline from roughly 7 million farms to just over 2 million. At the same time, acreage for each farm has increased while overall land acreage has remained level.[5]
   - The Agenda 2030 program states word-for-word that its goal is to build a more equitable distribution of the population in "balance with nature."

10. **Free education for all children in public schools. Abolition of children's factory labor in its present form. Combination of education with industrial produc-**

5 Roberto Ferdman, "The Decline of the Small American Family Farm in One Chart," The Washington Post, April 26, 2019, accessed September 02, 2020, https://www.washingtonpost.com/news/wonk/wp/2014/09/16/the-decline-of-the-small-american-family-farm-in-one-chart/)

tion, etc.
- The Department of Education has already enacted this policy.
- The goal of the communist Agenda 2030 plan is to turn education centers into work centers, with pre-selected careers based on the corporate-government elite's needs.

The Communist plan's core tenets run parallel with the goals of the United Nations' Agenda 2030. Their entire philosophy contradicts what many western philosophers have deemed "natural law." When society has a system based on theft—theft of individualism, theft of property, theft of knowledge and reason—it will inevitably clash with the core tendencies of mankind and the human spirit as a whole. In actuality, their philosophy is a breach of contract with our creator.

Cultural Marxism in America

The communists know this, which is why for their plan to work, they must reimagine the human spirit in their image, not God's or nature's. This is why the Democratic Party is waging a culture war against the core philosophies that helped build America's foundation. Class and racial conflict are essential for the communist economic structure to be successfully implemented. By dividing the citizenry among economic and racial lines, every citizen is pitted against one another so that citizens demand equality across the board. It will not be our current definition of equality where equal rights mean equal justice under the law. Instead, communism will ensure that everyone has an equal financial outcome from their labor. In reality, this environment will ensure that everyone is equally poor. By maintaining conflict among the populace, the elites maintain their stranglehold on all economic, political, and cultural life. The ultimate goal of Cultural Marxism is to confuse the natural order of things to destroy any other political or economic systems that stand in the way of the communist plan.

The term "Cultural Marxism" is somewhat of a misnomer as its philosophical foundation is a later interpretation of Karl Marx's version of communism. The political term is a label created by conservative political commentators in their observations of the political left's assembling of multiple strategies to enact their new socioeconomic order. Much of this strategy was developed from the Frankfurt School, or "Critical Theory," formed at the Institute for Social Research in Frankfurt, Germany, in 1923. The theory is mainly based on Hegel's dialectics, a social criticism, and interpretation of history. Claudio Corradetti of the University of Rome Tor Vergata notes:

> Critical theory has been strongly influenced by Hegel's notion of dialectics for the conciliation of socio-historical oppositions and Marx's theory of economy and society and the limits of Hegel's "bourgeois philosophy." Critical Theory has expanded Marxian criticisms of capitalist society by formulating patterns of social emancipatory strategies.[6]

Cultural Marxism can be defined as the social strategy necessary to implement a socialist or communist economic order. Corradetti continues:

> Dialectics, as a method of social criticism, was interpreted as following from the contradictory nature of capitalism as a system of exploitation…it was on the basis of such inherent contradictions that capitalism was seen to open up to a collective form of ownership of the means of production, namely, socialism.[7]

In other words, capitalism's inherent flaws can and should be exploited to enact a new communist order. The "social emancipatory strategies" mentioned focus on taking real or imagined social problems and placing them at the forefront of political discussion under the premise that socialism will lead to more individual freedom. In reality, this environment can never end as it is necessary to maintain the new communist order.

The world saw the effects of the Marxist strategy with the Russian Revolution in 1917. The October Revolution consisted mainly of class warfare between different political factions before and after the Bolsheviks victory in 1919. The strife continued with multiple grain shortages whereby the Bolsheviks would confiscate grain, land, and other property for the state. Of course, they would blame the wealthier peasants for these shortages. In reality, class conflict increased when the socialists took control.

---

[6] Claudio Corradetti, "Frankfurt School and Critical Theory," Internet Encyclopedia of Philosophy, accessed September 02, 2020, https://iep.utm.edu/frankfur/)

[7] Ibid.

Antonio Gramsci, a neo-Marxist from Italy, was not shy about their strategy to divide the populace to take full control. Without a doubt, identity politics truly was refined by the communists:

> the Communist Party cannot have competitors…In the present period of class struggle, the pseudo-revolutionary parties flower: Christian socialists (who have an easy hold amongst the peasant masses), the "real" socialists (ex-combatants, petit-bourgeois, all the restless spirits eager for whatever novelty), the individualist libertarians (noisy conventicles of unsatisfied vanities and capricious and chaotic tendencies). These parties have invaded the streets and deafen the electoral markets with their empty and endless phraseology, with stupefying and irresponsible promises, with noisy teasing of the lowest popular passions and of the narrowest selfishness.[8]

Although Gramsci claims that socialism "takes on the characteristics of a scolding hot sheet of metal, which can be sculpted in any way they [the socialists] choose,"[9] He recognizes that any political and philosophical theories that argue to the contrary should be soundly defeated with propaganda and force. The contradictions in his theories are obvious.

Today, Cultural Marxism has reimagined itself in the American image. America's political structure and demographical make-up have served as the perfect situation for socialists to take advantage of. Our diverse ethnic make-up and its history with slavery and segregation equate to an emancipatory struggle that can be used by the socialists for their purpose. Many foolishly believed that the election of Barack Obama as President had proven that America had finally moved on from its racist past. Yet, it seemed as if racial tensions increased in America after his election, and exponentially increased after the election of President Trump. Why?

The same tactics are being used in America 100 years later. Systemic racism that is racist policies sanctioned by the state no longer exists for minority populations in America. Multiple laws have been passed since the 1964 Civil Rights Act. In

[8] Antonio Gramsci, "The Development of the Revolution," Marxists.org, accessed September 02, 2020, https://www.marxists.org/archive/gramsci/1919/09/development-revolution.htm)

[9] Antonio Gramsci, "Revolution against Capital," Marxists.org, accessed September 02, 2020, https://www.marxists.org/archive/gramsci/1917/12/revolution-against-capital.htm)

reality, the laws have flipped to the opposite end of the spectrum. The only openly racist policies that exist specifically target white people on job and college applications under Affirmative Action programs. When viewing the current social environment in the United States, it as if the powers that be are stoking the perfect fires to cause unrest throughout the country. Every police brutality case highlighted by the mainstream media is never an open-and-shut case; it is always controversial. The stories have been cherry-picked to cause a specific reaction among the populace on both political sides of the aisle. Simultaneously, seemingly unrelated policy proposals are being attached to these causes for "social justice." You will never talk to a Black Lives Matter supporter who is not a socialist. You will never talk to a socialist that is not a proponent of the policies supported by the Agenda 2030 program.

When viewing the current events of 2020, it must be acknowledged that the COVID-19 response has been attached to the Black Lives Matter movement, removing President Trump from office, and the sustainable development movement. Marxist governors nationwide have attached COVID-19 policy proposals to sustainable development programs. Many perceive these events as isolated; however, when viewed with the communist strategy in mind, it becomes clear that these events are either being orchestrated or being used to create an American Bolshevik Revolution. The orchestrated chaos that America has seen in 2020 is unprecedented. One would truly have to trace history back to the American Civil War to find similar circumstances. The 1968 riots do not hold a candle to the level of organization and destruction seen in almost every major American city where Democrat Mayors and Governors hold power.

Communists have found their perfect weapon to enact their communist Agenda 2030 program: enrage black Americans nationwide. Enrage Hispanic Americans by falsely claiming President Trump is racist. Those that have bought into this ploy will now vote purely out of anger for an economic program that they falsely believe will cure all of their ills. To stop the Californication of America with the United Nations Agenda 2030 program, Cultural Marxism must be rooted out of the American political discussion. Any attempt to divide Americans along the lines of race, class, sexual preference, gender—is an attempt to

169

break apart the American family, the country, and our current way of life.

Conservative and libertarian Americans throughout the country can no longer sit on the sidelines. Claiming that "protesting is for liberals" is no longer an option, especially when this environment has led to an unemployment rate of over 20 percent. It is time for Americans to reject any part of American culture that has been co-opted to spread a message of hate. When the NBA, NFL, MLB chose to scribe "Black Lives Matter" across their stadiums, they chose to spread a divisive message that would make Martin Luther King, Jr. turn over in his grave. Americans should reject these attempts to divide and conquer the country by no longer buying a ticket and no longer watching the games on TV. When a Hollywood actor puts the "racist" scarlet letter on a conservative politician for merely disagreeing with an individual policy, Americans should no longer buy a ticket to the theater. When your employer insists on using the "proper pronouns" for your coworker who has a mental disorder, it is time to find a new career. Every moment we sacrifice our principles, the communist regime gains a firmer footing.

Americans must end their addiction to government regulation. Big government loves its regulatory power because it is a slam-dunk victory in any court. Before you have faced your accuser, you are already guilty. When people say, "common sense is a limited natural resource," they are right— it is our addiction to government intervention that has depleted it. It is not an exaggeration to say that there is a regulation for every human action taken throughout our daily lives. If Americans honor the golden rule and mind their own business, maybe we will become a self-reliant nation again. The precautionary principle and its arrogance to think we can play God must come to an end. The thought that it is the government's job to redistribute wealth must come to an end. When the average American sees that welfare is theft from their neighbor, we may be able to get along as a nation, as our founders intended. As Dr. Ron Paul said in his book *Liberty Defined*: "We are currently at a crossroads, deciding which political and economic path to take. It all boils down to two choices: either more government or less."[10]

---

[10] Ron Paul, Liberty Defined: The 50 Essential Issues That Affect Our Freedom (New York: Grand Central, 2012), p.57)

Removing the teeth of bureaucracies

To start reducing government size, we must remove the teeth of the bureaucracy by removing their enforcement power. Dr. Thomas Krannawitter proposes an exciting strategy that does just that in his political satire, *Save the Swamp: Career Guidebook for Budding Bureaucrats:*

> Members of Congress could, if they wanted, pass a law transforming all regulations issued by regulatory and administrative agencies into mere *suggestions* that have no legal force and no legal authority whatsoever unless and until those suggestions are approved by a vote of both chambers of Congress and signed into law by the President.[11]

This proposal is a creative way to slowly release the stranglehold bureaucracies have over the people. Still, the proposal places a significant amount of trust in our Congressmen, who also play a role in the revolving door between bureaucracies and corrupt business interests and have no term limits. Without a doubt, the proposal would have to become from popular demand from the American people. In the end, it would demand that the bureaucracies that are allowed to exist fall within the enumerated powers of the federal government.

The other large institution that has plagued the American political system is the private Federal Reserve bank. There have been numerous attempts from both Congressman Ron Paul and his son Senator Rand Paul to at least audit the Federal Reserve. All attempts have failed to look at the accounting ledger of the national bank for the world's largest economy. As Ron Paul likes to say, "the Federal Reserve is not Federal, and it is no longer a reserve." He says this because the bank is a private banking cartel of anonymous stakeholders, and as of 1973, we no longer back the dollar with gold. In reality, the Fed has now become a broker for the United States' massive $23 trillion debt. Since its inception in 1913, the Federal Reserve has devalued the dollar by 100 percent when compared to the value of gold.[12] At a

[11] Thomas L. Krannawitter, Save the Swamp: Career Guidebook for Budding Bureaucrats (Denver, CO: Speakeasy Ideas, 2017), p.271)

[12] Jan Nieuwenhuijs, "U.S. Dollar Devalues By 99% Vs. Gold In 100 Years - Gold Price Crosses $2,067," Seeking Alpha, August 08, 2020, accessed September 02, 2020, https://seekingalpha.com/article/4366155-u-s-dollar-devalues-99-vs-gold-in-100-years-gold-price-crosses-2067)

minimum, we must first audit the Federal Reserve, and then seek to end it altogether. Central banking has run the show in America for over 100 years with a track record of complete failure.

Secondarily, the spending binge that Congress has been on for the last fifty years must come to an end. Restricting the enforcement power of the unelected bureaucracies will surely help; however, it is clear that Congress needs further restriction on their actions through the power of a Constitutional amendment. It is time to force our leaders to balance their checkbooks as private citizens do.

After removing unnecessary bureaucracies, citizens must pay attention to what is going on at the local level. The Agenda 2030 sustainable development plan has found that working at the local level instead of the national level is more efficient. Californication of your state can be stopped if you keep organizations like ICLEI out of your local city council. Colorado's well-documented cultural and political transformation at California Marxists' hands should serve as a warning to other surrounding states. It is possible to create additional bike lanes and walkable communities without sacrificing property rights in the process. Any time city planners work to limit certain housing products on the market, it should be an immediate red flag. If your city council has adopted "smart city" plans, it is time to get active as soon as possible, for it may be too late.

Secession

Judiciaries from the local level to the Supreme Court have become the enforcement arm of the Agenda 2030 takeover. The realization that our entire judicial branch has morphed into an oligarchy has never been more apparent than under the Trump Presidency. The President has not been allowed to carry out his lawful duties, such as immigration enforcement, due to rogue Federal Judges in California. We can only hope that the long list of Federal Judges appointed by President Trump interprets the Constitution as written. The Federal 9th District Court's actions to remove the executive branch's vested power prove that their power has gone too far. Even at the local level, hundreds of district judges and district attorneys act like they are Gods. This is mostly due to a gross misinterpretation of judicial review

172

(Marbury v. Madison), which allows the Judiciary to rule specific actions by Congress or a President as unconstitutional. Those who agree with this sentiment would likely agree with Alexander Hamilton's views on the Judiciary in Federalist No. 78:

> Whoever attentively considers the different departments of power must perceive that, in a government in which they are separated from each other, the Judiciary, from the nature of its functions, will always be the least dangerous to the political rights of the Constitution; because it will be least in a capacity to annoy or injure them.[13]

Most constitutional scholars believe that once the Judiciary rules on an issue, the President and Congress must adhere to its ruling. However, the Constitution's best-kept secret is that the Congress and the Executive Branch can still act on their own accord. Our checks and balances system would demand that the People throw these politicians out of office through the process of impeachment or an election if they disagree with the actions that went against the court's decision.

The 1832 Supreme Court case *Worcester v. Georgia*, Chief Justice John Marshall, ruled that Georgia does not have the right to imprison members of the Cherokee Indian tribe. President Andrew Jackson, a staunch proponent of Indian removal, famously proclaimed: "John Marshall has made his decision, now let him enforce it."[14] The government's right to arrest Indians is not under dispute; the weight of Jackson's words are the most essential aspect of this case. Jackson highlights that the Supreme Court does not have an enforcement arm to impose their rulings—that power lies with the executive branch. This is the solution to the judicial tyranny that we all currently live under. This strategy will undoubtedly have a ripple-effect on lower rulings. By ignoring the Supreme Court's decisions, it takes the debate directly to the American people. Simultaneously, we must start paying attention to our local judges, who wield more power than any city councilman or congressman. The criminal justice system in America is so corrupt that it may be necessary to clean the house on all judges until proper order is restored. When the 9th District rules that President Trump cannot enforce our nation's

---

[13] Alexander Hamilton, The Federalist Papers, No. 78, (Mineola, NY: Dover Publications, 2014), p.379)

[14] Thomas A. Donovan, At Sidebar, report, September 2012, accessed September 2, 2020, https://www.fedbar.org/wp-content/uploads/2012/09/sidebar sep12-pdf-1.pdf)

immigration laws, he should simply go ahead and do it regardless of the court's ruling. It is time to let the American people decide, not an oligarch in black robes.

The official Democrat strategy plans for the 2020 election have suggested it may be necessary to secede if Trump is re-elected in 2020. The Federalists argued that this is not an option if we want to maintain a strong union. History has shown that the Federalists were wrong on the one dilemma for which we separated from England for, specifically, the size and power of the national government. They failed to put necessary restrictions on the Federal government, placing the majority of their focus on the states. Their failure to address this risk can be surmised in their opinions on secession and the potential abuse of power at the hands of the Judiciary. If California wants to secede from the Union after Trump's re-election, the neighboring states should strongly consider listening to California's concerns. Suppose we revisit tort law and general contract law. In that case, we know that any union should be voluntary. If it is not, the actors involved will rebel in other ways, causing further interruption and destruction to the Union, forcing the nation into a slow, painful death.

History has shown that the Anti-Federalists were right in their critique of the Constitution. We have seen the government grow too large, and we are seeing local governments and state governments in open rebellion against the Federal government. It is time as countrymen that we consider breaking up in order to preserve the Union. Although our Constitution forbids it, the Amendment process may allow for a path to allow secession through an arduous process that requires the poise of stable minds. If we are allowed to admit states to the Union, we should let states leave if they choose. When examining the laws in states like California and Oregon, it is apparent that they have disregarded the federal Constitution already; this is especially true as it relates to the 1st and 2nd Amendments.

The Declaration of Independence's main intention is to remind us that we have the right to absolve the current government if it becomes an immediate threat to our liberty. The Federalists would argue this should be done through the election process. They are correct; however, if oppression continues, there must be a revolutionary kill-switch. We must begin to con-

174

sider the arguments of the Anti-Federalists over the arguments of the Federalists, as it has become clear that their Constitutional cures continually fail as government becomes more extensive and more oppressive.

Ron Paul describes the concept of secession as something that is multi-faceted. The term does not simply mean a state deciding to leave their national government; it also applies to citizens choosing to defy individual actions taken by the government. He argues that the concept could be applied to a situation where U.S. Army troops simply say no to unconstitutional war:

> We need to build up enough enthusiasm and determination and belief [in the concept of nullification] that those individuals who are required to or drafted to or bribed into going off and fighting these senseless wars [simply] refuse to go.[15]

He continues to state that secession becomes a natural reaction when the failures of big government continue to mount:

> It is coming to an end. The FED is going to end. There's going to be a de-facto secession movement, the states are going to refuse to listen to some of the laws, we have seen tremendous success already with states saying no to unconstitutional drug laws...I think the American people are waking up to it, and so as far as I'm concerned, the more the merrier.[16]

By allowing state sovereignty to flourish, individual sovereignty will follow. If a state wants to separate from the Union fully, the rest of the States should consider their arguments, especially if the majority of the people within that state support it.

Californication is the American realization and implementation of classic Marxism. It is the process of transformation of each state in America in accordance with the United Nations Agenda 2030 communist program. We are witnessing the rise of the American technocracy in our reaction to COVID-19 combined with the sustainable development platform. In effect, the structure will be defined by a new form of medical tyranny. It is a direct attack on western civilization and America's political and cultural foundations. Simultaneously, it is an attack on what we all know as "the American Dream." By uprooting Cultural Marx-

---

15 Speech by Ron Paul, Secession and Liberty, Mises Institute, February 2, 2015, accessed September 2, 2020, https://www.youtube.com/watch?v=g36Ef5Fvkok, 24:00)

16 Speech by Ron Paul, Secession and Liberty, Mises Institute, February 2, 2015, accessed September 2, 2020, https://www.youtube.com/watch?v=g36Ef5Fvkok, 33:00)

ism from our society and adhering to the Constitutional solutions available to us, we can restore confidence in America's institutions. By recognizing that our most sacred rights in America can be protected through respecting our private property rights, we will live vicariously and responsibly. America was once the most reliant nation on earth. Whether the slogan is "Restore America Now" or "Make America Great Again," America's future will be defined by its choice for more freedom—or more government.

Bibliography

Primary Sources

Karl Marx and Friedrich Engels. "The German Ideology," in *Classics of Political & Moral Philosophy*, ed. Steven M. Cahn. New York, Oxford University Press, 2012.

Karl Marx and Friedrich Engels. "Manifesto of the Communist Party," in *Classics of Political & Moral Philosophy*, ed. Steven M. Cahn. New York, Oxford University Press, 2012.

Gramsci, Antonio. "Revolution against Capital." Marxists.org. Accessed September 02, 2020. https://www.marxists.org/archive/gramsci/1917/12/revolution-against-capital.htm.

Gramsci, Antonio. "The Development of the Revolution." Marxists.org. Accessed September 02, 2020. https://www.marxists.org/archive/gramsci/1919/09/development-revolution.html.

Hamilton, Alexander, James Madison, and John Jay. *The Federalist Papers*. Mineola, NY: Dover Publications, 2014.

Ketcham, Ralph. *The Anti-Federalist Papers and the Constitutional Convention Debates*. New York, NY: Signet Classic, 2003.

Locke, John. "Second Treatise of Government," in *Classics of Political & Moral Philosophy*, ed. Steven M. Cahn. New York, Oxford University Press, 2012.

Plato. "Republic," in *Classics of Political & Moral Philosophy*, ed. Steven M. Cahn. New York, Oxford University Press, 2012.

Rousseau, Jean-Jacques. "Discourse on the Origin of Inequality," in *Classics of Political & Moral Philosophy*, ed. Steven M. Cahn. New York, Oxford University Press, 2012.

Smith, Adam. "The Wealth of Nations," in *Classics of Political*

& *Moral Philosophy*, ed. Steven M. Cahn. New York, Oxford
University Press, 2012.

United States Constitution. 1787.

United States Declaration of Independence. 1776.

Secondary Sources

"2010 Climate Action Plan Status Report." City of Fort Collins ,
July 2011. https://www.fcgov.com/climateaction/pdf/2010CAP-
StatusReport.pdf?1509983351.

"2018 Ballots Received." Colorado Secretary of State, June 27,
2018. https://www.sos.state.co.us/pubs/newsRoom/pressReleas-
es/2018/20180627BallotsReceivedByAgePartyGender.pdf.

"A $1,000 Emergency Would Push Many Americans into
Debt." CNBC. CNBC, January 23, 2019. https://www.cnbc.
com/2019/01/23/most-americans-dont-have-the-savings-to-cov-
er-a-1000-emergency.html.

Abramson, Dustin, Derrick, and Joseph Edwin. "CRYPTOCUR-
RENCY SYSTEM USING BODY ACTIVITY DATA." patent-
scope.wipo.int, March 26, 2020. https://patentscope.wipo.int/
search/en/detail.jsf?docId=WO2020060606&tab=PCTBIBLIO.

Ackerman, Spencer. "CIA Chief: We'll Spy on You Through
Your Dishwasher." Wired. Conde Nast, June 3, 2017. https://
www.wired.com/2012/03/petraeus-tv-remote/.

Allen, Jaclyn. "Sheriff: Bill Could Have Saved Deputy's Life."
The Denver Channel. KMGH, April 24, 2018. https://www.
thedenverchannel.com/news/360/douglas-county-sheriff-red-
flag-bill-could-have-saved-deputy-parrishs-life.

"American Families Face a Growing Rent Burden." The Pew
Charitable Trusts. Accessed April 12, 2020. https://www.

pewtrusts.org/en/research-and-analysis/reports/2018/04/ameri-can-families-face-a-growing-rent-burden.

Anglen, Robert. "Cliven Bundy Is Free, but Standoff Case Isn't Over: What You Need to Know," Azcentral, February 08, 2018. AZ Central. Accessed June 15, 2019. https://www.azcentral. com/story/news/local/arizona-investigations/2018/01/04/cliv-en-ammon-bundy-ranch-standoff-trial-what-know-nevada-ranch-ing-mistrial/997221001/.

"Artspace Loveland Arts Campus." Artspace. Accessed March 19, 2020. https://www.artspace.org/loveland#leasing-section.

"Asian Cities Climate Change Resilience Network (ACCCRN): The Rockefeller Foundation." The Rockefeller Foundation. Accessed December 11, 2011. http://www.rockefellerfoundation. org/what-we-do/current-work/developing-climate-change-resil-ience/acccrn-partners.

Bartels, Lynn. "Climate Change Guru Tom Steyer Donates Big Bucks to Help Mark Udall." The Denver Post. The Denver Post, April 27, 2016. https://www.denverpost.com/2014/05/22/climate-change-guru-tom-steyer-donates-big-bucks-to-help-mark-udall/.

Bartels, Lynn. "Colorado Republicans Split Delegate Votes between Romney, Unified Paul and Santorum Supporters." The Denver Post. The Denver Post, May 2, 2016. https://www. denverpost.com/2012/04/14/colorado-republicans-split-dele-gate-votes-between-romney-unified-paul-and-santorum-support-ers/.

Batura, Paul. "Paul Batura: Will Coronavirus Make Handshaking Go Extinct after Thousands of Years? Trump and Others Won-der." Fox News. FOX News Network, March 14, 2020. https:// www.foxnews.com/opinion/coronavirus-alternatives-hand-shake-paul-batura.

Baumann, Joella. "Colorado Supreme Court To Decide Fate Of Ban On High-Capacity Magazines." Colorado Public Ra-dio. Colorado Public Radio, July 1, 2019. https://www.cpr.

179

org/2019/04/23/colorado-supreme-court-to-decide-fate-of-ban-on-high-capacity-magazines/.

Black, Edwin. "The Horrifying American Roots of Nazi Eugenics." *History News Network*. George Mason University, 25 Nov. 2003. (History News Network) Accessed December 11, 2011. (http://hnn.us/articles/1796.html)

Bode, Karl. "Your Smart Electricity Meter Can Easily Spy On You, Court Ruling Warns." Vice. Vice, August 24, 2018. https://www.vice.com/en_us/article/j5n3pb/your-smart-electricity-meter-can-easily-spy-on-you-court-ruling-warns.

Bryan, Bob. "The US National Debt Just Pushed Past $22 Trillion - Here's How Trump's $2 Trillion in Debt Compares with Obama, Bush, and Clinton." Business Insider. Business Insider, February 20, 2019. https://www.businessinsider.com/trump-national-debt-deficit-compared-to-obama-bush-clinton-2019-2.

Brzezinski, Zbigniew. Between Two Ages: Americas Role in the Technetronic Era. Westport, CT: Greenwood Press, 1982.

Burness, Alex. "Defying Trump, Boulder Declares Itself a Sanctuary City." Daily Camera. Boulder Daily Camera, January 3, 2017. https://www.dailycamera.com/2017/01/03/defying-trump-boulder-declares-itself-a-sanctuary-city/.

Camarota, Steven A. "The Impact of Immigration on California." CIS.org. Center for Immigration Studies, July 1, 1998. https://cis.org/Report/Impact-Immigration-California.

Camarota, Steven A., and Karen Zeigler. "63% Of Non-Citizen Households Access Welfare Programs." CIS.org. Center for Immigration Studies, November 20, 2018. https://cis.org/Report/63-NonCitizen-Households-Access-Welfare-Programs.

Cameron, Darla, Dan Keating, and Armand Emamdjomeh. "Analysis | Where Do Federal Workers Live?" The Washington Post. WP Company, August 30, 2018. https://www.washingtonpost.com/graphics/2018/politics/federal-workers/.

Carley, Sanya, Denvil Duncan, John D. Graham, Saba Siddiki, and Nikolaos Zirogiannis. "A Macroeconomic Study of Federal and State Automotive Regulations." Indiana University, March 2017. https://oneill.indiana.edu/doc/research/working-groups/auto-report-032017.pdf.

"Carnegie Institution for Science Homepage." Carnegie Institute for Science. Accessed December 11th, 2011. http://carnegie-science.edu.

Chandler, Dave. "Mr. Mayor, It's Still a $30 Land Deal." Arvada Press. Colorado Community Media, June 12, 2018. https://arvadapress.com/stories/mr-mayor-its-still-a-30-land-deal,263318.

"Cheyenne Metropolitan Area Pedestrian Plan." Cheyenne MPO. Cheyenne Metropolitan Planning Organization, August 2010. https://www.plancheyenne.org/mpo-project/cheyenne-metropolitan-area-pedestrian-plan/.

Choi, Jung Hyun, Jun Hyun Zhu, and Laurie Hyun Goodman. "The State of Millennial Homeownership." Urban Institute, July 18, 2018. https://www.urban.org/urban-wire/state-millennial-homeownership.

Christie, Les. "Foreclosures up a Record 81% in 2008." CNNMoney. Cable News Network, January 15, 2009. https://money.cnn.com/2009/01/15/real_estate/millions_in_foreclosure/.

Cilluffo, Anthony, A.W. Geiger, and Richard Fry. "More U.S. Households Are Renting than at Any Point in 50 Years." Pew Research Center. Pew Research Center, July 19, 2017. https://www.pewresearch.org/fact-tank/2017/07/19/more-u-s-households-are-renting-than-at-any-point-in-50-years/.

"Climategate 2.0? More Emails Leaked From Climate Researchers." Fox News. FOX News Network, December 18, 2014. https://www.foxnews.com/science/climategate-2-0-more-emails-leaked-from-climate-researchers.

Collins, Mike. "The Big Bank Bailout." Forbes. Forbes Magazine, July 14, 2015. https://www.forbes.com/sites/mikecollins/2015/07/14/the-big-bank-bailout/#7b5403e92d83.

"Colorado Governor Signs Sweeping Police Accountability Bill into Law. Here's How It Will Change Law Enforcement." The Colorado Sun. Accessed August 18, 2020. https://coloradosun.com/2020/06/19/colorado-police-accountability-bill-becomes-law/.

"Colorado Adopts California Emissions Standards." Colorado Springs Gazette. Colorado Springs Gazette, February 14, 2020. https://gazette.com/news/colorado-adopts-california-emissions-standards/article_75cf2d4e-e9fc-11e8-9f4b-371bc967a46c.html.

"Colorado Population 1900-2019." MacroTrends. Accessed March 18, 2020. https://www.macrotrends.net/states/colorado/population.

Complete Colorado. "Steyer's Got Company: Billionaire George Soros Makes a Play for Colorado's State Legislature." Complete Colorado - Page Two, September 18, 2017. https://pagetwo.completecolorado.com/2016/08/02/steyer-soros-colorado-state-legislature/.

Confessore, Nicholas, and Julia Preston. "Soros and Other Liberal Donors to Fund Bid to Spur Latino Voters." The New York Times. The New York Times, March 10, 2016. https://www.nytimes.com/2016/03/10/us/politics/george-soros-and-other-liberal-donors-to-fund-bid-to-spur-latino-voters.html.

Corradetti, Claudio. "Frankfurt School and Critical Theory." Internet Encyclopedia of Philosophy. Accessed September 02, 2020. https://iep.utm.edu/frankfur/.

"CPI for All Urban Consumers, New Vehicles in U.S. City Average." U.S. Bureau of Labor Statistics. U.S. Bureau of Labor Statistics. Accessed February 22, 2020. https://data.bls.gov/pdq/SurveyOutputServlet.

"Current Employment Statistics - CES (National)." U.S. Bureau of Labor Statistics. Accessed August 18, 2020. https://www.bls.gov/ces/.

Daugherty, Owen. "Homelessness Rates Increase in US for Second Straight Year." TheHill. The Hill, December 17, 2018. https://thehill.com/blogs/blog-briefing-room/news/421684-homelessness-rates-increase-in-us-for-second-straight-year.

"Denver Becomes 11th City in Colorado to Raise Tobacco Age to 21." Tobacco Free Colorado. October 04, 2019. Accessed August 18, 2020. https://www.tobaccofreeco.org/product/vaping-and-ecigs/denver-becomes-11th-city-in-colorado-to-raise-tobacco-age-to-21/.

"Depopulation Quotes." The Sovereign Independent. Accessed December 11, 2011. http://www.sovereignindependent.com/?p=2574.

Denver Smart City. Accessed March 19, 2020. https://www.denvergov.org/content/denvergov/en/denver-smart-city.html.

DeSilver, Drew. "For Most Americans, Real Wages Have Barely Budged for Decades." Pew Research Center. Pew Research Center, August 7, 2018. http://www.pewresearch.org/fact-tank/2014/10/09/for-most-workers-real-wages-have-barely-budged-for-decades/.

Dietz, Robert. "Multifamily Construction Data: 2nd Quarter 2019." Eye On Housing, August 19, 2019. http://eyeonhousing.org/2019/08/multifamily-construction-data-2nd-quarter-2019/.

Donovan, Thomas A. At Sidebar. Report. September 2012. Accessed September 2, 2020. https://www.fedbar.org/wp-content/uploads/2012/09/sidebar-sep12-pdf-1.pdf.

Elliott, Dan. "Colorado Governor Signs Major Overhaul of Oil and Gas Rules." AP NEWS. Associated Press, April 17, 2019. https://apnews.com/ca4a57d130b64c658901f4d4b773c9ab.

Emmons, William R. "The End Is in Sight for the U.S. Foreclosure Crisis." Federal Reserve Bank of St. Louis. Federal Reserve Bank of St. Louis, December 14, 2016. https://www.stlouisfed. org/publications/housing-market-perspectives/2016/the-end-is-in-sight-for-the-us-foreclosure-crisis#endnote1

Emrath, Paul. "Government Regulation in the Price of a New Home." NAHB. National Association of Homebuilders, May 2, 2016. https://www.nahbclassic.org/generic.aspx?genericContentID=250611.

Emrath, Paul, and Caitlin Walter. "Regulation: Over 30 Percent of the Cost of a Multifamily Development." NAHB. National Association of Home Builders, June 12, 2018. https://www.nahbclassic.org/generic.aspx?genericContentID=262391.

"Event 201, a Pandemic Exercise to Illustrate Preparedness Efforts," Event 201. Center for Health Security, January 25, 2020. Accessed September 3, 2020. http://www.centerforhealthsecurity. org/event201/.

"Evidence of BLM's Deadly Abuse of Animals Taken from Bundy Ranch," 21st Century Wire, April 22, 2014. 21st Century Wire. Accessed June 15, 2019. https://21stcenturywire. com/2014/04/16/exclusive-evidence-of-blms-deadly-abuse-of-animals-taken-from-bundy-ranch/.

Fadulu, Lola. "Homelessness Rises 2.7 Percent, Driven by California's Crisis, Report Says." The New York Times. The New York Times, December 20, 2019. https://www.nytimes. com/2019/12/20/us/politics/homelessness-trump-california.html.

Ferdman, Roberto. "The Decline of the Small American Family Farm in One Chart." The Washington Post. April 26, 2019. Accessed September 02, 2020. https://www.washingtonpost.com/ news/wonk/wp/2014/09/16/the-decline-of-the-small-american-family-farm-in-one-chart/.

Fernholz, Tim. "SpaceX Wins Lucrative New Contracts to Fly

GPS and Earth-Imaging Satellites." Quartz. Quartz, March 15, 2018. https://qz.com/1229463/elon-musks-spacex-wins-lucra-tive-new-contracts-to-fly-gps-and-earth-imaging-satellites-for-the-us-air-force/.

Ferrier, Pat. "Innosphere Plans $18M Expansion in Fort Collins, Denver." Coloradoan. The Coloradoan, December 8, 2017. https://www.coloradoan.com/story/money/busi-ness/2017/12/08/innosphere-plans-18-m-expansion-fort-collins-denver/922755001/.

"Finance." DOW Jones Industrial Average Chart. Google. Ac-cessed March 17, 2020. https://www.google.com/finance.

Fingerhut, Hannah. "Partisanship and Political Animosity in 2016." Pew Research Center for the People and the Press, De-cember 31, 2019. http://www.people-press.org/2016/06/22/parti-sanship-and-political-animosity-in-2016.

Frank, John. "Colorado Hits a New Milestone with Unaffiliated Voters and Busts the Myth about Its Even Partisan Split." The Colorado Sun. The Colorado Sun, December 26, 2019. https://coloradosun.com/2019/12/26/colorado-voter-registration-unaffil-iated-voters-2020-election/.

Frank, John. "Colorado Republicans Cancel Presidential Vote at 2016 Caucus." The Denver Post. The Denver Post, April 22, 2016. https://www.denverpost.com/2015/08/25/colorado-republi-cans-cancel-presidential-vote-at-2016-caucus/.

Friedman, Zack. "78% Of Workers Live Paycheck To Paycheck." Forbes. Forbes Magazine, January 11, 2019. https://www.forbes.com/sites/zackfriedman/2019/01/11/live-paycheck-to-pay-check-government-shutdown/.

Fryar, Cheryl, Jeffrey Hughes, and Kirsten Herrick. "Fast Food Consumption Among Adults in the United States, 2013–2016." CDC, National Center for Health Statistics , October 2018. https://www.cdc.gov/nchs/data/databriefs/db322-h.pdf.

Funk, Josh. "Virus Closes Some Meat Plants, Raising Fears of Shortages." AP NEWS. Associated Press, April 13, 2020. https://apnews.com/d855667c811d3d9810883e05702288ad.

Gates, Bill. "Bill Gates on Energy: Innovating to Zero!" TED, February, 2010. Accessed December 11, 2011. http://www.ted.com/talks/bill_gates.html.

"General Welfare," JRank Articles. Accessed August 18, 2020. https://law.jrank.org/pages/7116/General-Welfare.html.

Golodryga, Brianna. ABC News. ABC News Network, January 12, 2011. https://abcnews.go.com/Business/2010-record-29-million-foreclosures/story?id=12602271.

Goodman, Christopher J, and Steven M Mance. "Employment Loss and the 2007–09 Recession: an Overview." Bureau of Labor Statistics , April 2011. https://www.bls.gov/opub/mlr/2011/04/art1full.pdf.

Gruver, Tim. "States Consider Taxing Drivers by the Mile despite Privacy Concerns." POLITICO. POLITICO, June 9, 2017. https://www.politico.com/story/2017/06/08/states-consider-taxing-drivers-by-the-mile-despite-privacy-concerns-239336.

Gross, Daniel. "Why Sell Toll Roads to Foreign Companies?" Slate Magazine. March 29, 2006. Accessed September 20, 2020. https://slate.com/business/2006/03/why-sell-toll-roads-to-foreign-companies.html.

Hains, Tim. "Ocasio-Cortez: 'The World Is Going To End In 12 Years If We Don't Address Climate Change.'" RealClearPolitics, January 22, 2019. https://www.realclearpolitics.com/video/2019/01/22/ocasio-cortez_the_world_is_going_to_end_in_12_years_if_we_dont_address_climate_change.html.

Hains, Tim. "Tom Steyer Says He Became The Biggest Donor In Politics To Advocate For Getting Money Out Of Politics." RealClearPolitics. RealClearPolitics, November 26, 2017. https://www.realclearpolitics.com/video/2017/11/26/tom_steyer_says_

he_became_the_biggest_donor_in_politics_to_advocate_for_get-
ting_money_out_of_politics.html.

Hansen, Randall, and Desmond S King. Sterilized by the State:
Eugenics, Race, and the Population Scare in Twentieth-Century
North America. Cambridge: Cambridge University Press, 2013.

Harris, Ricki. "Elon Musk: Humanity Is a Kind of 'Biological
Boot Loader' for AI." Wired. Conde Nast, n.d. https://www.
wired.com/story/elon-musk-humanity-biological-boot-loader-ai/.

"History shows that trade made easy, "U.S. Has Lost 5 Million Manufacturing Jobs since 2000," CNNMoney. CNN,
March 29, 2016. accessed March 5, 2020. http://money.cnn.
com/2016/03/29/news/economy/us-manufacturing-jobs/

"How the Dems Won Colorado." The Denver Post. The Denver
Post, April 8, 2010. https://www.denverpost.com/2010/04/08/
how-the-dems-won-colorado/.

"How the Mile-High City Is Embracing Smart City Solutions."
CTIA. Accessed March 19, 2020. https://www.ctia.org/news/
how-the-mile-high-city-is-embracing-smart-city-solutions.

"International Council of Local Environmental Initiatives, 1995."
ICLEI - Local Governments for Sustainability. Accessed December 11, 2011. http://www.iclei.org.

Iserbyt, Charlotte. "Charlotte Iserbyt - Common Core - Save
Long Island Forum 1/18/14." YouTube. We Are Change CT ,
January 25, 2014. https://www.youtube.com/watch?v=OA5zStX-
dGlo.

Kachmar, Kala, and Darcy Costello. "Louisville Is Forcing Unwilling Coronavirus Patients to Self-Isolate. Is It Right?" Journal.
Louisville Courier Journal, April 3, 2020. https://www.couri-
er-journal.com/story/news/2020/03/31/louisville-circuit-court-an-
kle-bracelets-noncompliant-coronavirus-patients/5094594002/.

Kaelber, Lutz. "California Eugenics." Eugenics: Compulsory

Sterilization in 50 American States. University of Vermont, March 4, 2009. https://www.uvm.edu/~lkaelber/eugenics/CA/ CA.html.

Karlik, Michael. "Background Checks for Guns Triple as Wait Times Cross Federal Threshold." Colorado Politics, March 30, 2020. https://www.coloradopolitics.com/coronavirus/ background-checks-for-guns-triple-as-wait-times-cross-federal-threshold/article_72d2a81c-6e0f-11ea-81d5-47623c7fe29a.html.

Keating, Joseph C, and Scott Haldeman. "Joshua N Haldeman, DC: the Canadian Years, 1926-1950." The Journal of the Canadian Chiropractic Association, September 1995, 172–86. https://www.ncbi.nlm.nih.gov/pmc/articles/PMC2485067/pdf/ jcca00035-0046.pdf.

Kerch, Steve. "2009 Foreclosures Hit Record High." Market-Watch. MarketWatch, January 14, 2010. https://www.market-watch.com/story/foreclosures-top-record-in-2009-no-end-in-sight-2010-01-14.

Kotecki, Peter. "54 Photos of New York City Microapartments Show How Tiny Living Can Be Glamorous - or Disappointing." Business Insider. Business Insider, December 26, 2018. https:// www.businessinsider.com/photos-nyc-micro-apartments-2018-10#this-129-million-apartment-in-midtown-manhattan-is-starved-for-storage-but-it-includes-several-crafty-design-elements-like-a-hidden-pantry-6.

Krannawitter, Dr. Thomas, Speakeasy Ideas Newsletter. "Is the Will of the Majority Reasonable?"Feb 5, 2019. Accessed March 29, 2020. Email.

Krannawitter, Thomas L. *Save the Swamp: Career Guidebook for Budding Bureaucrats*. Denver, CO: Speakeasy Ideas, 2017.

Krasno, Jean E. *The United Nations: Confronting the Challenges of a Global Society*. Lynne Rienner, 2004.

Kriebel, D., J. Tickner, P. Epstein, J. Lemons, R. Levins, E. L.

Loechler, M. Quinn, R. Rudel, T. Schettler, and M. Stoto. "The Precautionary Principle in Environmental Science." Environmental Health Perspectives. September 2001. Accessed August 18, 2020. https://www.ncbi.nlm.nih.gov/pmc/articles/PMC1240435/.

Kroft, Steve, and Dinesh D'Souza. "George Soros 60 Minutes Interview." CBS, 1999. https://www.youtube.com/watch?v=X9t-KvasRO54&t=7s.

Kudialis, Chris. "Why Cliven Bundy Tried to Pay Grazing Fees to Clark County, Not BLM," Las Vegas Sun, November 07, 2017. Las Vegas Sun. Accessed June 15, 2019. https://lasvegassun.com/news/2017/nov/07/why-cliven-bundy-sent-grazing-fees-clark-county/.

Kuhl, Stefan. Nazi Connection Eugenics, American Racism, and German National Socialism. Cary: Oxford University Press, USA, 2014.

Kundu, Bishwajit. "Uncanny Similarity of Unique Inserts in the 2019-NCoV Spike Protein to HIV-1 gp120 and Gag ." BIORxRv, February 2, 2020. https://www.biorxiv.org/content/10.1101/2020.01.30.927871v1.full.pdf.

"Labor Force Participation Rate," U.S. Bureau of Labor Statistics. Accessed March 12, 2020, https://data.bls.gov/

Lamb, Kailyn. "Safety Advocates Seek to Stop Bicycle Fatality Trend." Centennial Citizen. Colorado Community Media, September 3, 2019. https://centennialcitizen.net/stories/safety-advocates-seek-to-stop-bicycle-fatality-trend,285622.

Laxen, Jacob. "Fort Collins Named Third Best Biking City in Nation." Coloradoan. The Coloradoan, October 11, 2018. https://www.coloradoan.com/story/life/2018/10/11/fort-collins-named-countrys-third-best-biking-city/1602373002/.

"LEED-Certified Buildings Are Often Less Energy-Efficient Than Uncertified Ones." Forbes. Forbes Magazine, May 1, 2014. https://www.forbes.com/sites/realspin/2014/04/30/leed-cer-

tified-buildings-are-often-less-energy-efficient-than-uncerti-
fied-ones/#3bdb4f125544.

Lopez, Ashley. "Super Tuesday Could Show Just How Blue
Texas Is Turning." NPR. NPR, March 2, 2020. https://www.npr.
org/2020/03/02/810401130/super-tuesday-could-show-just-how-
blue-texas-is-turning.

"Louisiana Pastor Arrested after Holding Services despite
Stay-at-Home Order, Report Says." WWL. WWL, March 31,
2020. https://www.wwltv.com/article/news/health/coronavirus/
louisiana-pastor-arrested-after-holding-services-despite-coro-
navirus-order-report-says/289-4394a314-3c13-4047-95d7-e4f6
5f517752.

Lynne, Stacy. "Plan Cheyenne Town Hall." Plan Cheyenne
Town Hall. Accessed March 1, 2020. https://www.youtube.com/
watch?v=iEABMOFdqAc.

"M&A Poll: Voters Overwhelmingly Support Term Limits for
Congress." McLaughlin & Associates. Accessed August 18,
2020. https://mclaughlinonline.com/2018/02/08/ma-poll-voters-
overwhelmingly-support-term-limits-for-congress/.

Maybee, Julie E. "Hegel's Dialectics." Stanford Encyclopedia
of Philosophy. Stanford University, June 3, 2016. https://plato.
stanford.edu/entries/hegel-dialectics/.

Mayer, Chris, Karen Pence, and Shane M. Sherlund. "The
Rise in Mortgage Defaults." Federal Reserve, November 1,
2008. https://www.federalreserve.gov/pubs/feds/2008/200859/
200859pap.pdf.

Miller, Blair. "Michael Bloomberg Unveils Anti-Gun Violence
Policy at Aurora Town Hall." thedenverchannel . KMGH,
December 6, 2019. https://www.thedenverchannel.com/news/
local-news/michael-bloomberg-set-to-unveil-anti-gun-violence-
policy-at-aurora-town-hall.

Moore, Stephen. "The Growth of Government in America:

Stephen Moore." FEE Freeman Article. April 01, 1993. Accessed August 18, 2020. https://fee.org/articles/the-growth-of-government-in-america/.

Morgan, Edmund S. "The American Revolution: Revisions in Need of Revising." William & Mary Quarterly, 3rd series, 14, no. 1 (1957), p. 11.

Mosher, Steven W. "Opinion: Don't Buy China's Story: The Coronavirus May Have Leaked from a Lab." New York Post. New York Post, March 5, 2020. https://nypost.com/2020/02/22/dont-buy-chinas-story-the-coronavirus-may-have-leaked-from-a-lab/.

Munnell, Alicia H, and Matthew S Rutledge. "The Effects of the Great Recession on the Retirement Security of Older Workers ." National Poverty Center , March 1, 2013. http://npc.umich.edu/publications/u/2013-03-npc-working-paper.pdf.

Nieuwenhuijs, Jan. "U.S. Dollar Devalues By 99% Vs. Gold In 100 Years - Gold Price Crosses $2,067." Seeking Alpha. August 08, 2020. Accessed September 02, 2020. https://seekingalpha.com/article/4366155-u-s-dollar-devalues-99-vs-gold-in-100-years-gold-price-crosses-2067.

Ochsner, Nick. "Toll Road Troubles: Politicians, Experts Point to Cintra's History as Cautionary Tale for NC." Https://www.wbtv.com. February 12, 2016. Accessed September 20, 2020. https://www.wbtv.com/story/31177025/toll-road-troubles-politicians-experts-point-to-cintras-history-as-cautionary-tale-for-nc/.

"Our Local Government Members & Regional and Higher Education Affiliates." ICLEI USA. Accessed March 19, 2020. https://icleiusa.org/membership/.

Parvini, Sarah. "L.A. Threatens to Shut off Water, Power of Businesses Breaking Coronavirus Rules." Los Angeles Times. Los Angeles Times, March 25, 2020. https://www.latimes.com/california/story/2020-03-25/la-water-power-businesses-coronavirus-closure-rules.

Paul, Jesse. "10 People in Colorado May Have Cast Two Ballots in 2016 Election, While 38 Might Have Also Voted in Another State, Study Says." The Denver Post. The Denver Post, September 15, 2017. https://www.denverpost.com/2017/09/15/colorado-2016-improper-voting-study/.

Paul, Ron. *Liberty Defined: the 50 Essential Issues That Affect Our Freedom*. New York: Grand Central, 2012.

Paul, Ron. "Secession and Liberty." February 2, 2015. Accessed September 2, 2020. https://www.youtube.com/watch?v=g36Ef-5Fvkok.

Paulson, Henry M. "Opinion | The Coming Climate Crash." The New York Times. The New York Times, June 21, 2014. http://www.nytimes.com/2014/06/22/opinion/sunday/lessons-for-climate-change-in-the-2008-recession.html.

"People in Denver Forced to Sell Affordable Housing They Didnt Know They Bought." KUSA, March 21, 2018. https://www.9news.com/article/news/local/next/people-in-denver-forced-to-sell-affordable-housing-they-didnt-know-they-bought/73-530761758.

Peters, Jeremy W. "Bloomberg Plans a $50 Million Challenge to the N.R.A." The New York Times. The New York Times, April 16, 2014. https://www.nytimes.com/2014/04/16/us/bloomberg-plans-a-50-million-challenge-to-the-nra.html.

Phillips, Noelle. "Violent Crime up 25 Percent in Colorado since 2013, Latest CBI Report Shows." The Denver Post. The Denver Post, September 28, 2018. https://www.denverpost.com/2018/09/28/colorado-crime-data/.

Poole, Stephen. "Benefit Corporations: Expansion of the Public-Private Fascist State, Part 4." Freedom Advocates, August 17th, 2011. Accessed December 1, 2011. http://www.freedomadvocates.org/articles/illegitimate_government/benefit_corporations:_expansion_of_the_public-private_fascist_state,_ part_4_20110817449.

"Prism Collection Documents." The Washington Post. Accessed
September 20, 2020. https://www.washingtonpost.com/wp-srv/
special/politics/prism-collection-documents/.

"Protecting Private Property Rights from Regulatory Takings."
Cato Institute, December 15, 2012. https://www.cato.org/pub-
lications/congressional-testimony/protecting-private-proper-
ty-rights-regulatory-takings.

Reid, Carlton. "San Francisco Bans Cars From Market Street
124 Years After Bicyclists Called For Primacy." Forbes. Forbes
Magazine, January 26, 2020. https://www.forbes.com/sites/carl-
tonreid/2020/01/26/san-francisco-bans-cars-from-market-street-
124-years-after--bicyclists-called-for-primacy/#6afd40a25387.

Rental Housing Progams. Report. October 2018. Accessed
September 2, 2020. https://www.nilc.org/wp-content/up-
loads/2016/03/rental_housing_1005.pdf.

Residential Provisions of the 2018 International Energy Conservation Code, Residential Provisions of the 2018 International
Energy Conservation Code § (2018). https://www.energycodes.
gov/sites/default/files/becu/2018_IECC_residential.pdf.

Ridler, Keith. "Is Idaho Turning a Little Blue? Primary Might
Provide Clues." AP NEWS. Associated Press, March 5, 2020.
https://apnews.com/45486c6b90f7cae1b237248fef3f05bf.

Root, Wayne Allyn. "COMMENTARY: Illegal Immigrants
Have Turned California into the American Nightmare." Review
Journal. Las Vegas Review-Journal, November 9, 2018. https://
www.reviewjournal.com/opinion/opinion-columns/wayne-allyn-
root/commentary-illegal-immigrants-have-turned-california-in-
to-the-american-nightmare/.

Rose, Joel. "The Latest Immigration Crackdown May Be Fake
Social Security Numbers." NPR. NPR, March 29, 2019. https://
www.npr.org/2019/03/29/707931619/social-security-administra-

tion-plans-to-revive-no-match-letters.

Rosenthal, Jack. "A Terrible Thing to Waste." The New York Times. The New York Times, July 31, 2009. https://www.ny-times.com/2009/08/02/magazine/02FOB-onlanguage-t.html.
Rosiak, Luke, and Richard Pollock. "EXography: Worst-of-the-Worst in Energy Efficiency Earn LEED's Highest --- and Meaningless --- Rating." Washington Examiner, January 14, 2014. https://www.washingtonexaminer.com/exography-worst-of-the-worst-in-energy-efficiency-earn-leeds-highest-and-mean-ingless-rating.

Schiff, Peter. "The Next Financial Crash Is Coming (2020)." Cambridge House International , 2018. https://www.youtube.com/watch?v=WD2zcyfwdJ4.

Schwartz, Peter. "Scenarios for the Future of Technology and International Development." Rockefeller Foundation , June 2010. https://www.rockefellerfoundation.org/news/publications/scenarios-future-technology.

"SDSG." Sustainable Development Strategies Group. Accessed December 11, 2011. http://www.sdsg.org/about-us/.

Seibler, John-Michael. "Commerce Clause Just Keeps On Ex-panding." The Heritage Foundation. Accessed August 18, 2020. https://www.heritage.org/government-regulation/commentary/commerce-clause-just-keeps-expanding.

"SNAP Data Tables." USDA. Accessed March 17, 2020. https://www.fns.usda.gov/pd/supplemental-nutrition-assistance-pro-gram-snap.

Sommers, Christina Hoff. The War against Boys: How Mis-guided Feminism Is Harming Our Young Men. New York, NY: Simon & Schuster, 2001.

Starnes, Todd. "Facebook Using Company Run by Former CNN Staffer to Target Conservatives." Todd Starnes. Todd Starnes, February 24, 2020. https://www.toddstarnes.com/values/facebook-using-company-run-by-former-cnn-staffer-to-target-conser-vatives/.

Stolerman, Katherine. "The American Eugenics Movement: A Study of the Dispersal and Application of Racial Ideologies." Aisthesis, November 2, 2017. https://pubs.lib.umn.edu/index.php/aisthesis/article/view/49.

Sustainable Development Strategies Group. Accessed December 11, 2011. http://www.sdsg.org/about-us/.

Svaldi, Aldo. "Colorado Is No. 3 in the Country for Rising Car Insurance Premiums. Here's Why." The Denver Post. The Denver Post, February 28, 2018. https://www.denverpost.com/2018/02/27/colorado-car-insurance-premiums-rise/.

Tabachnik, Sam. "With 80,000 New Residents, Colorado Is the Seventh-Fastest Growing State in the U.S." The Denver Post. The Denver Post, December 24, 2018. https://www.denverpost.com/2018/12/24/colorado-population-growth/.

"The American Middle Class Is Losing Ground." Pew Research Center's Social & Demographic Trends Project, December 31, 2019. http://www.pewsocialtrends.org/2015/12/09/the-american-middle-class-is-losing-ground/.

"The Appeal." 5G Appeal, March 4, 2019. http://www.5gappeal.eu/scientists-and-doctors-warn-of-potential-serious-health-ef-fects-of-5g/.

Thompson, Don. "California Moves to Consider Reparations for Slavery." SFGate. August 30, 2020. Accessed September 02, 2020. https://www.sfgate.com/news/article/Califor-nia-moves-to-consider-reparations-for-15524833.php.

"Total Assets of the Federal Reserve." Board of Governors of the Federal Reserve System. Federal Reserve. Accessed March 17, 2020. https://www.federalreserve.gov/monetarypolicy/bst_re-centtrends.htm.

"U.S. National Debt Clock: Real Time." U.S. National Debt Clock: Real Time. Accessed March 17, 2020. https://www.usdebtclock.org/.

"Unemployment Rate," FRED Economic Data. Federal Reserve of St. Louis. Accessed March 5, 2020. https://fred.stlouisfed.org/search?st=Unemployment Rate for United States.

Wadhams, Nick, and Jennifer Jacobs. "China Concealed Extent of Virus Outbreak, U.S. Intelligence Says." Bloomberg.com. Bloomberg, April 1, 2020. https://www.bloomberg.com/news/articles/2020-04-01/china-concealed-extent-of-virus-outbreak-u-s-intelligence-says.

"Walkable and Livable Communities Institute Homepage." Walklive. Accessed December 11, 2011. http://www.walklive.org/.

Weiss, Haley. "Why You're Probably Getting a Microchip Implant Someday." The Atlantic. Atlantic Media Company, September 21, 2018. https://www.theatlantic.com/technology/archive/2018/09/how-i-learned-to-stop-worrying-and-love-the-microchip/570946/.

Weissmann, Jordan. "60 Years of American Economic History, Told in 1 Graph." The Atlantic. Atlantic Media Company, September 6, 2012. https://www.theatlantic.com/business/archive/2012/08/60-years-of-american-economic-history-told-in-1-graph/261503/.

Wheelock, David C. "The Federal Response to Home Mortgage Distress: Lessons from the Great Depression." Federal Reserve Bank of St. Louis Review. Federal Reserve Bank of St. Louis, 2008. https://files.stlouisfed.org/files/htdocs/publications/review/08/05/Wheelock.pdf, p.137.

"Who We Are." Who is ICLEI | ICLEI Global. Accessed March 19, 2020. http://old.iclei.org/index.php?id=8.

"Wildlands Network." Wildlands Network. Accessed December

11, 2011. http://www.twp.org/.

Wingerter, Justin. "Soros Family, Private Prison Company Inject Thousands into U.S. Senate Race." The Denver Post. The Denver Post, February 7, 2020. https://www.denverpost.com/2020/02/07/fundraising-2020-senate-hickenlooper-gardner/.

Zimmer, Amy. "Who's Moving Into and Out of Colorado?" Colorado Virtual Library, December 17, 2018. https://www.coloradovirtuallibrary.org/resource-sharing/state-pubs-blog/whos-moving-into-and-out-of-colorado/.

Executive Orders, Congressional Legislation & Official Reports

America 2050: A Prospectus. Report. September 2005. Accessed September 21, 2020. https://rpa.org/work/reports/america-2050-prospectus.

"Agenda 21." United Nations, 1992. https://sustainabledevelopment.un.org/content/documents/Agenda21.pdf.

"Budget of the U.S Government." Office of Management and Budget. Accessed August 21, 2020. https://www.govinfo.gov/app/collection/budget/2021/BUDGET-2021-TAB.

Cameron Gulbransen Kids Transportation Safety Act of 2007, 1216, 110th Cong., 2nd sess. Introduced in House December 19, 2007. https://www.govinfo.gov/content/pkg/STATUTE-122/pdf/STATUTE-122-Pg639.pdf.

"CRS Report: Welfare Spending the Largest Item in the Federal Budget," 112th (2011). S. Rep.

The State of Homelessness in America, The State of Homelessness in America § (2019). https://www.whitehouse.gov/wp-content/uploads/2019/09/The-State-of-Homelessness-in-America.

pdf.

"Executive Order 12852-Presidents Council on Sustainable Development." Executive Order 12852-Presidents Council on Sustainable Development | The American Presidency Project, June 29, 1993. http://www.presidency.ucsb.edu/ws/index.php?pid=61547.

Exec. Order No. 13575, 3 C.F.R. (2011).

"Governor Gavin Newsom Issues Stay at Home Order." California Governor, March 21, 2020. https://www.gov.ca.gov/2020/03/19/governor-gavin-newsom-issues-stay-at-home-order/.

Henry, Meghan, Anna Mahathey, Tyler Morrill, Anna Robinson, Azim Shivji, and Rian Watt. "The 2018 Annual Homeless Assessment Report (AHAR) to Congress." The U.S. Department of Housing and Urban Development, December 2018. https://files.hudexchange.info/resources/documents/2018-AHAR-Part-1.pdf.

"President Donald J. Trump Is Committed To Safeguarding America's Vital Communications Networks And Securing 5G Technology." The White House. The United States Government, March 12, 2020. https://www.whitehouse.gov/briefings-statements/president-donald-j-trump-committed-safeguarding-americas-vital-communications-networks-securing-5g-technology/.

"Transforming Our World: the 2030 Agenda for Sustainable Development, Sustainable Development Knowledge Platform." United Nations. United Nations, September 25, 2015. https://sustainabledevelopment.un.org/post2015/transformingourworld.

Verizon 5G Ultra Wideband service coming to Denver in 2019. Accessed March 19, 2020. https://www.denvergov.org/content/denvergov/en/mayors-office/newsroom/2019/verizon-5g-ultra-wideband-service-coming-to-denver-in-2019.html.

Court Cases

DISTRICT OF COLUMBIA et al. v. HELLER, 554 U.S. Report 570 (June 26, 2008).

Naperville Smart Meter Awareness v. City of Naperville. 900 F.3d 521 (7th Circuit, 2018).

U.S. Supreme Court. 1935. United States v. Butler, syllabus, 401 U.S 1.

.

www.ingramcontent.com/pod-product-compliance
Lightning Source LLC
La Vergne TN
LVHW051052080426
835508LV00019B/1830